W9-DDA-457

Inside SCIENCE

Natural Disaster Research

Other titles in the *Inside Science* series:

Inside SCIENCE

Natural
Disaster
Research

Lydia Bjornlund

ReferencePoint
Press®

San Diego, CA

© 2012 ReferencePoint Press, Inc.
Printed in the United States

For more information, contact:
ReferencePoint Press, Inc.
PO Box 27779
San Diego, CA 92198
www.ReferencePointPress.com

LIBRARY OF CONGRESS CATALOGING-IN-PUBLICATION DATA

Bjornlund, Lydia D.
  Natural disaster research / Lydia Bjornlund.
    p. cm. -- (Inside science)
  Includes bibliographical references and index.
  ISBN-13: 978-1-60152-236-8 (hardback)
  ISBN-10: 1-60152-236-3 (hardback)
  1. Natural disasters--Research. I. Title.
  GB5005.B54 2011
  363.34--dc23
                                                    2011039700

Contents

Foreword

In 2008, when the Yale Project on Climate Change and the George Mason University Center for Climate Change Communication asked Americans, "Do you think that global warming is happening?" 71 percent of those polled—a significant majority—answered "yes." When the poll was repeated in 2010, only 57 percent of respondents said they believed that global warming was happening. Other recent polls have reported a similar shift in public opinion about climate change.

Although respected scientists and scientific organizations worldwide warn that a buildup of greenhouse gases, mainly caused by human activities, is bringing about potentially dangerous and long-term changes in Earth's climate, it appears that doubt is growing among the general public. What happened to bring about this change in attitude over such a short period of time? Climate change skeptics claim that scientists have greatly overstated the degree and the dangers of global warming. Others argue that powerful special interests are minimizing the problem for political gain. Unlike experiments conducted under strictly controlled conditions in a lab or petri dish, scientific theories, facts, and findings on such a critical topic as climate change are often subject to personal, political, and media bias—whether for good or for ill.

At its core, however, scientific research is not about politics or 30-second sound bites. Scientific research is about questions and measurable observations. Science is the process of discovery and the means for developing a better understanding of ourselves and the world around us. Science strives for facts and conclusions unencumbered by bias, distortion, and political sensibilities. Although sometimes the methods and motivations are flawed, science attempts to develop a body of knowledge that can guide decision makers, enhance daily life, and lay a foundation to aid future generations.

The relevance and the implications of scientific research are profound, as members of the National Academy of Sciences point out in the 2009 edition of *On Being a Scientist: A Guide to Responsible Conduct in Research:*

Some scientific results directly affect the health and well-being of individuals, as in the case of clinical trials or toxicological studies. Science also is used by policy makers and voters to make informed decisions on such pressing issues as climate change, stem cell research, and the mitigation of natural hazards. . . . And even when scientific results have no immediate applications—as when research reveals new information about the universe or the fundamental constituents of matter—new knowledge speaks to our sense of wonder and paves the way for future advances.

The *Inside Science* series provides students with a sense of the painstaking work that goes into scientific research—whether its focus is microscopic cells cultured in a lab or planets far beyond the solar system. Each book in the series examines how scientists work and where that work leads them. Sometimes, the results are positive. Such was the case for Edwin McClure, a once-active high school senior diagnosed with multiple sclerosis, a degenerative disease that leads to difficulties with coordination, speech, and mobility. Thanks to stem cell therapy, in 2009 a healthier McClure strode across a stage to accept his diploma from Virginia Commonwealth University. In some cases, cutting-edge experimental treatments fail with tragic results. This is what occurred in 1999 when 18-year-old Jesse Gelsinger, born with a rare liver disease, died four days after undergoing a newly developed gene therapy technique. Such failures may temporarily halt research, as happened in the Gelsinger case, to allow for investigation and revision. In this and other instances, however, research resumes, often with renewed determination to find answers and solve problems.

Through clear and vivid narrative, carefully selected anecdotes, and direct quotations each book in the *Inside Science* series reinforces the role of scientific research in advancing knowledge and creating a better world. By developing an understanding of science, the responsibilities of the scientist, and how scientific research affects society, today's students will be better prepared for the critical challenges that await them. As members of the National Academy of Sciences state: "The values on which science is based—including honesty, fairness, collegiality, and openness—serve as guides to action in everyday life as well as in research. These values have helped produce a scientific enterprise of unparalleled usefulness, productivity, and creativity. So long as these values are honored, science—and the society it serves—will prosper."

Important Events in Natural Disaster Research

1752
Benjamin Franklin's experiments with lightning lead to the invention of the lightning conductor, an early tool for predicting storm-related disasters.

1946
The Pacific Tsunami Warning Center is established in Honolulu, Hawaii.

1846
Thomas R. Robinson invents the spinning cup anemometer to measure wind speed.

1906
Following the Great San Francisco Earthquake, the city establishes new building codes requiring buildings to withstand a set amount of ground shaking.

1820   **1860**   **1900**   **1940**

1805
Sir Francis Beaufort develops a chart to estimate wind speed. The Beaufort scale is still used today.

1860s
Weather stations begin to be established in North America, Europe, and other parts of the world to collect information from a wide area to forecast the weather.

1935
Charles F. Richter invents a scale to measure the magnitude of earthquakes. The scale becomes known as the Richter scale.

1885
The first seismograph for measuring earth tremors is created by British geologist John Milne.

1441
Korea's king Sejong orders the development of a rain gauge to forecast floods and droughts.

1904
Norwegian physicist Vilhelm Bjerknes publishes a paper suggesting a mathematical approach that would make it possible to forecast the weather, earning him a name as the father of modern meteorology.

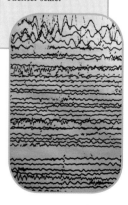

1949
Edward M. Brooks of St. Louis University discovers that tornadoes usually form within larger masses of rotating air known as mesocyclones.

1979
The Federal Emergency Management Agency (FEMA) is created by executive order to bring under one umbrella disparate natural and manmade disaster–related programs.

2009
The world's foremost tornado experts convene in the Midwest as part of VORTEX2, the largest tornado study in the world.

2005
Hurricane Katrina hits the Gulf Coast, becoming the most destructive storm in US history. The events that unfold prompt researchers to explore the nature of US preparedness and response systems.

2011
A tsunami triggered by an earthquake off the coast of Japan kills 22,000 people, destroys entire communities, and forces the shut-down of nuclear power plants in Fukushima.

1958
Japanese volcanologist Kiyoo Mogi introduces a means (the Mogi Model) for modeling the changes in a volcano caused by the internal pressure of magma.

1997
FEMA releases the first edition of HAZUS, a geographic information system–based natural hazard loss estimation software package.

1950   **1965**   **1980**   **1995**   **2010**

1977
Congress passes legislation creating the National Earthquake Hazards Reduction Program, a research and implementation partnership focused on reducing the risks to life and property from earthquakes.

2010
Teams of scientists from around the world map the geology of Haiti in an attempt to guide rebuilding following an earthquake that levels most of Port-au-Prince.

1950
The first weather satellite, TIROS-1, is sent into orbit; John von Neumann and colleagues at the Institute for Advanced Study in Princeton, New Jersey, create the first computer weather forecast.

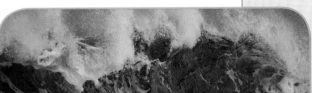

2004
In the Indian Ocean an earthquake-triggered tsunami kills upward of 230,000 people, prompting the extension of the Pacific Tsunami Warning Center to the Indian Ocean.

Why Study Disasters?

On December 26, 2004, a massive earthquake occurred under the Indian Ocean off the west coast of Sumatra, Indonesia. Scientists later confirmed that the earthquake was among the most powerful ever recorded. Because it occurred in the Indian Ocean, the earthquake itself caused only minor damage. The real danger lay in the series of waves that were triggered by the earthquake.

On that beautiful, sunny day in Indonesia, the resorts lining the islands were crowded with tourists enjoying their winter holiday. Locals went about their business as usual. No one was prepared for the tsunami that raced across the ocean and slammed into the shore. The mammoth waves reached almost 100 feet (30.5 m) high as they crashed into the islands of the Indian Ocean and dragged people, trees, and entire buildings back out into the ocean. Indonesia was hit the worst, but the tsunami wreaked havoc in 14 different countries, not only in the Indian Ocean but on the eastern coast of Africa as well. In fact, eight people lost their lives in South Africa—more than 5,000 miles (8,047 km) from the epicenter of the earthquake. Within hours, the tsunami had claimed the lives of at least 230,000 people, making it one of the deadliest natural disasters in history.

epicenter

The exact location on the earth's surface above the breaking of rocks or other disturbance that causes an earthquake.

Jose Borrero of the University of Southern California Tsunami Research Center was one of the first scientists to witness the aftermath of the disaster. In his journal he describes the devastation in the Aceh province of Northern Sumatra, Indonesia, which was one of the hardest hit areas:

The tsunami had deposited debris . . . miles from the open ocean. The words "war zone" barely did the scene justice, but it wasn't even close to what I would see next over the next few days. . . .

We took the cars over to a riverfront area. This scene was truly mind-blowing. Boats were twisted and smashed and piled up on top of the bridge where we were standing. I couldn't stop saying "Oh my god. . . ." There were piles of debris 20 or 30 [feet] high, there were bodies in the piles, legs and arms sticking out. Based only on the smell, there had to be three bodies I didn't see for every one I did see.[1]

The Indian Ocean tsunami caught the attention of the world. Amateur videos on the evening news brought home the terror of the event, showing people one minute casually strolling along the beach and the next being dragged out to sea. Aerial photos following the disaster showed the immensity of the devastation, while interviews with victims

Survivors of the 2004 Indian Ocean tsunami that killed hundreds of thousands of people rummage through the devastated city of Banda Aceh in Indonesia. The tsunami spawned new research aimed at a more complete understanding of the events that lead to natural disasters and better ways of protecting people in their path.

and families of those missing brought home the toll it took on humans. The disaster became what disaster researcher Claire B. Rubin calls a "focusing event,"[2] spawning new research intended to provide insight into what happened and inform public policy. Scientists from many different fields were among the people who asked what could be done to prevent such tragedy from occurring again in the future. "I still can't shake the feeling of sadness for the people of Indonesia and around the world who suffered in this disaster," writes Borrero on his last day in Indonesia. "However, I am also completely in awe of the force of nature."[3]

Research Before and After

Following a natural disaster like the Indian Ocean tsunami, scientists like Borrero go to the scene to try to learn what happened. They visit the site to identify the areas and structures that were hardest hit. They take measurements to determine how far away the earthquake was. Where exactly did the earthquake occur? Why did it happen when it did? What was the cause of the disruption? These are just a few of the questions researchers seek to answer following a quake.

Some of the research following an event focuses also on the impact a natural disaster has had on the earth and its processes. Volcanic eruptions have been known to cause short-term climate changes that may impact global warming. A violent hurricane may change the shoreline. A flood may change the flow of water. An earthquake may trigger volcanic eruptions or other quakes called aftershocks or huge tsunamis halfway around the world. Better understanding of how the hazards relate to one another and impact the earth's natural processes can help predict future events.

Most disaster research is focused on using this knowledge to save lives in the future. Researchers seek clues about how to predict an earthquake before it occurs. They look for ways to detect even minor ground shaking and to improve communication so people have more time to respond. Experience shows that improving warning systems is critical to saving lives. Prior to the 2004 Indian Ocean tsunami, a network was in place—the Pacific Tsunami Warning Center based in Honolulu—to detect tsunamis in the Pacific Ocean. The Indian Ocean tsunami focused attention on the need to extend the detection and warning system to areas beyond the existing network. Researchers also focused attention on the need for better education of populations at risk of a tsunami. "The strong shaking by the earthquake should have been nature's warning for the local residents that a tsunami was imminent and they could have run to higher ground to save their lives," writes disaster expert George Pararas-Carayannis. "A simple program of public education and awareness of the potential hazard could have saved many lives in the immediate area."[4]

Disaster Disciplines

Earthquakes and tsunamis are just two of the hazards studied by scientists. Natural disaster research focuses also on volcanoes, hurricanes, tornadoes, floods, and a wide range of other natural hazards. As with any field of science, curiosity drives much of the research, but to this curiosity is added the reality of what is at stake. "We're here to save lives and property,"[5] says a member of the hurricane research team of the National Oceanic and Atmospheric Administration (NOAA).

geophysics

The branch of earth science that deals with the physics of the earth, particularly focusing on the structure of rocks at and below the earth's surface.

Scientists from many different fields contribute to the understanding of natural hazards and disasters. Knowledge of geology and geophysics, for instance, is critical to understanding the causes of disasters such as earthquakes and volcanoes, while knowledge of meteorology provides insight into weather-related disasters such as hurricanes and tornadoes. Oceanographers have played an increasing role in helping people understand how currents and changes in oceanic conditions, including temperature and tides, influence a tropical storm or hurricane. Ecologists too are playing an increasing role in disaster research, contributing valuable information about how the earth's natural processes work together and how human changes to the environment may increase hazard-related risk. Meanwhile, National Aeronautics and Space Administration (NASA) scientists—once focused on looking outward toward space—are increasingly focused on Earth, using the views from space to help understand natural disasters.

Computer scientists have played a critical role in advancing the capability of these and other scientists to test their theories and link past events to forecasting events of the future. Finally, psychologists, sociologists, and other social scientists study human behavior before, during, and after a disaster for clues about how to influence behavior in a way that reduces loss of life.

What Are Natural Disasters?

Since the beginning of time, people have experienced the sudden unleashing of the earth's energy. Earthquakes shook the ground below. Violent storms raged overhead. Archeologists have uncovered evidence that entire communities were wiped out by these and other natural forces. Perhaps most famous is the destruction of Pompeii. At the height of the Roman Empire, Pompeii was a bustling, prosperous city about 8 miles (13 km) from Mount Vesuvius. In 79 AD, however, Mount Vesuvius erupted. For two days it spewed hundreds of pounds of molten rock and ash, burying Pompeii. Citizens tried to run but were stopped in their tracks by overwhelming surges of heat, which scientists estimate could have been upward of 450°F (232°C). Thick clouds of ash clogged the air. By the end of the violent eruption, Pompeii was lost under layers of ash and rock called tephra.

> **tephra**
>
> Fragments of ash, dust, and rock ejected from a volcano during an eruption.

Although human communities have changed dramatically over 2,000 years, the earth has not. Scientists warn that volcanoes still have the power to bury nearby cities. And as the population grows, natural disasters become ever more deadly; the more people who live in one place, the greater the likelihood that a disaster will cause catastrophic damage and deaths.

Defining a Natural Disaster

Earthquakes and volcanoes are reminders that the earth is constantly shifting and moving deep underground. Changes in the earth's atmosphere that define climate and weather can also spawn hurricanes, tornadoes, floods, drought, and other forms of severe weather. These natural disasters are the result of the ever changing nature of the earth and the environment in which people live.

Experts differentiate between natural hazards and natural disasters. A hazard is something that has the potential to cause harm. The volcano that overshadowed Pompeii was a natural hazard. A natural disaster, on the other hand, occurs when the hazard results in widespread destruction or distress; that is, when the volcano erupts to destroy a nearby community or when a tornado touches ground where people are living.

Researchers also differentiate natural disasters from human-caused disasters, such as a terrorist attack or the failure of a nuclear power plant. However, the line between the two types of disasters is sometimes blurred. For instance, a flood can be caused by human error or technological breakdown, such as the failure of a dam or levee. Natural disasters can also cause other types of hazards. In 2011 an earthquake off the coast of Japan caused a tsunami. The tsunami struck the coast just minutes after the earthquake, killing more than 22,000 people. The disaster was far from over, however, as explosions and leaks of radioactive gas at a nuclear power plant in Fukushima forced more than 2,000 residents to evacuate the area. Traces of radiation were found in water pouring from the reactors into water in Tokyo and the ocean.

Natural disasters vary widely in both cause and effect. Some disasters, such as an earthquake or landslide, happen with no warning, but scientists often track the formation of a tropical storm or hurricane for days prior to its landfall. Similarly, the damage done by an earthquake or volcano tends to be fairly local, especially when compared to the devastation caused by a far-moving hurricane or cluster of tornadoes. Furthermore, no two storms—or volcanoes or earthquakes—are alike. Each responds to the unique environment in which it exists.

Earthquakes

Some disasters, such as earthquakes, are sudden and violent, starting and ending within minutes. "Earthquakes are so scary because you don't have any warning," says Allan Lindh, a scientist with the U.S. Geological Survey (USGS). "It's the only thing besides a nuclear war [in which] one minute you're living in a beautiful city and ten seconds later it's flat."[6]

Experts say that more than a million earthquakes occur throughout the world each year. Most are minor tremors caused by rocks breaking far below the ground or under the ocean floor, where they cannot be felt by humans. But roughly once a year a major earthquake causes catastrophic devastation.

Following a quake, scientists measure the shaking and give the earthquake a number that shows its intensity. This is called the earthquake's magnitude. The magnitude scale starts at 1.0. At magnitude 1.0, the trembling is so minor that it cannot be felt by humans. Each number up from 1 represents 10 times as much power or force. Shaking that reaches a magnitude of 5.0 or 6.0 is strong enough break dishes and cause cracks in walls. Major earthquakes are typically defined as those that are of magnitude 8.0 or higher. Major earthquakes release energy equivalent to several nuclear bombs. On average, the world witnesses one or two earthquakes of this size each year.

An earthquake's magnitude tells nothing about the damage that results. A magnitude 6.0 earthquake under a population center may be far more devastating than a magnitude 8.0 quake in a deserted area. In addition, some earthquakes take place farther below the earth's crust than others do. All else being equal, a shallower earthquake will cause more damage than a deeper one.

Earthquakes are among the deadliest of all natural disasters. Most deaths from an earthquake are caused by collapsing buildings. Aftershocks—small quakes caused by the initial disturbance—often trigger additional fires, landslides, or floods. Sometimes aftershocks occur within hours or minutes of the initial quake, but with a large earthquake aftershocks sometimes continue for days, weeks, or even months.

Tectonic Plate Theory

Earthquakes are a reminder that the earth is constantly changing. Studying the history of the earth over several millennia pointed to clues that the earth's crust was moving—a theory that became known as continental drift. A century ago, a German scientist named Alfred Wegener theorized that the collision of continents or other pieces of the earth's crust led to the formation of mountains: When the leading edge of the continent encountered resistance, it folded upward to form mountain ranges and volcanoes, he theorized.

Wegener's ideas were not well received by the scientific community at the time, but more recent study of the earth has proved his theory to be sound. In the 1960s scientists developed instruments that allowed them to map the surface of the earth under water. These maps revealed a system of oceanic ridges where molten rock rises from below the crust and hardens into new crust. At these ridges is where volcanoes are located.

Today, scientists have shown that the earth's crust is made up of enormous slabs of rock called tectonic plates that fit together like a jigsaw puzzle. Under the earth's crust lies the mantle, a layer of hot rocks. The rocks cool near the edge of the plates, and the hotter rock in the middle begins to rise. This causes the plates to move in different directions. When the plates collide, they release energy. The waves of energy—called seismic waves—cause the ground to shake.

The world's most violent earthquakes occur at the fault, which is where the tectonic plates meet. In the United States, the area generally considered to be most vulnerable to a major earthquake lies where the Pacific Plate and the North American Plate meet, at the San Andreas Fault, which lies under some of California's largest cities. The movement of these plates was responsible for several large earthquakes, including the 1906 San Francisco earthquake, which was among the United States' most deadly.

> **tectonic plates**
>
> Large pieces of the earth's crust that move relative to one another, causing seismic and volcanic activity.

Tsunamis

The movement of tectonic plates also helps explain tsunamis. A tsunami, which means "harbor wave" in Japanese, is a series of giant waves that occur with little warning. When an earthquake happens on the ocean floor, the seismic waves can form into huge ocean waves. Tsunamis are often caused when one tectonic plate slides under another, a process called subduction. The 2004 Indian Ocean tsunami and the 2011 tsunami that struck Japan were both the result of subduction.

> **subduction**
>
> The process in which one tectonic plate slides under another, often causing an earthquake, tsunami, or volcanic eruption.

The islands of the Pacific are most vulnerable to tsunamis, but they have also threatened other parts of the world. In fact, the tallest wave ever recorded was a tsunami in Lituya Bay, Alaska, in 1958. The Alaska tsunami occurred near a fault line, but it was not caused by an earthquake. Rather, it was the result of a landslide in which a huge mass of rock plunged approximately 3,000 feet (914 m) into the waters of Gilbert Inlet. The impact generated a huge wave that uprooted millions of trees and removed all vegetation from elevations 1,720 feet (524 m) above sea level.

The Development of a Tsunami

Subduction zones are potential tsunami locations

Most tsunamis are caused by earthquakes generated in a subduction zone, an area where an oceanic plate is being forced down into the mantle by plate tectonic forces. The friction between the subducting plate and the overriding plate is enormous. This friction prevents a slow and steady rate of subduction and instead the two plates become stuck.

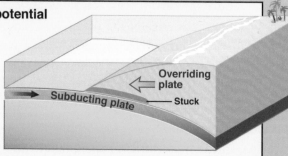

Overriding plate

Subducting plate

Stuck

Accumulated seismic energy

As the stuck plate continues to descend into the mantle the motion causes a slow distortion of the overriding plate. The result is an accumulation of energy very similar to the energy stored in a compressed spring. Energy can accumulate in the overriding plate over a long period of time—decades or even centuries.

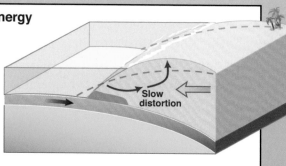

Slow distortion

Earthquake causes tsunami

Energy accumulates in the overriding plate until it exceeds the frictional forces between the two stuck plates. When this happens, the overriding plate snaps back into an unrestrained position. This sudden motion is the cause of the tsunami—because it gives an enormous shove to the overlying water. At the same time, inland areas of the overriding plate are suddenly lowered.

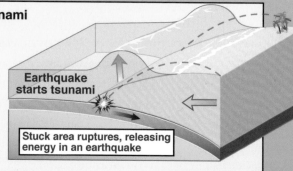

Earthquake starts tsunami

Stuck area ruptures, releasing energy in an earthquake

Tsunami races away from the epicenter

The moving wave begins travelling out from where the earthquake has occurred. Some of the water travels out and across the ocean basin, and, at the same time, water rushes landward to flood the recently lowered shoreline.

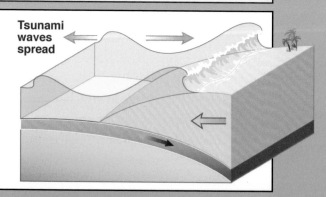

Tsunami waves spread

18

Volcanoes

Understanding tectonic plates also helps explain why some places have more volcanoes than others. Sometimes the pressure of tectonic plates forces the edge of the plate upward to form a ridge. Volcanoes are formed when unusually hot magma pushes up from a layer of magma deep within the earth. The magma forms a hot spot that is just under the earth's crust. The hot spot is stationary, but the tectonic plates above it are moving. As a tectonic plate moves over the hot spot, the magma creates a string of volcanoes. The Hawaiian Islands were formed in this manner.

Most of the world's volcanoes are located at the edges of tectonic plates where plates are moving apart and new crust is being formed, particularly where the Pacific Plate meets many surrounding plates. The area surrounding the Pacific Ocean, which has become known as the "Ring of Fire," is the most seismically and volcanically active zone in the world. Volcanoes also can be pushed up in the middle of a plate, although this is much less common. The volcanoes in Europe, including Mount Vesuvius, were formed in the center of a plate. Scientists say that many undiscovered volcanoes likely exist along the ocean floor.

fault

Fracture in the earth's crust at the boundary between two tectonic plates slowly grinding past each other or moving away from one another.

Volcanoes can be a beautiful part of the landscape when they are quiet, but their tranquil beauty belies the fiery turmoil underground. Beneath the earth's surface, hot magma continues to move and to melt the rocks around it. The hot magma also seeks to rise above cooler rock. When the pressure becomes intense, the magma pushes upward and collects in chambers below the surface. If a crack opens up in the crust, the molten rock spews out at the earth's surface. In general, the longer a volcano has been inactive, the larger and more explosive the eruption. In 1991, Mount Pinatubo, a volcano in the Philippines, erupted after being dormant for more than 600 years. For nine hours, the volcano spewed molten rock more than 12 miles (19 km) into the atmosphere—one of the largest and most violent eruptions of the century. The volcano continued to pour forth gases and particulates for three weeks following this initial blast.

The eruption of Pinatubo had a global impact. Millions of tons of sulphur dioxide were released into the atmosphere, blocking the sun's rays from reaching the earth. In 1992 and 1993, the average temperature in the Northern Hemisphere was reduced by about 1°F, (0.5 to 0.6°C)

Almost one month after the cataclysmic June 1991 eruption of Mount Pinatubo in the Philippines, smoke and ash continue to rise from the volcano. The eruption was one of the largest and most violent in the past century.

and the entire planet was cooled 0.7°F to 0.9°F (0.4 to 0.5°C). Scientists also believe these climate changes contributed to other natural disasters, including devastating flooding of the Mississippi River in 1993 and an extended period of drought in Africa. Studies also showed that the eruption increased the size of the hole in the ozone layer. This layer of the stratosphere absorbs most of the sun's ultraviolet radiation, and some scientists believe its erosion is contributing to global warming.

Not all volcanic activity results in an eruption. Sometimes magma oozes to the top of a volcano and forms a pool of lava. When the lava mixes with water from rain or melting snow, it overflows the crater at the top of the volcano and begins to slide down the side of the volcano, burying everything in its path. These landslides of volcanic debris

lahars

Landslides or mudflows of volcanic debris.

are called lahars. Although lahars may be less spectacular and sudden than a more explosive eruption, they can be just as deadly. In 1985 lahars from the Nevado del Ruiz volcano in the Andes Mountains buried the town of Armero, Colombia, and killed 25,000 people.

Characterizing Levels of Unrest

A common way of looking at volcanoes is by the frequency or recentness of their eruptions. Volcanoes that are considered active are those that erupt regularly or have erupted recently. Volcanoes that were once active but have not erupted for hundreds or even thousands of years are considered dormant, and those that are not expected to erupt again are considered extinct. Volcanologists—experts who study volcanoes—spurn these classifications, however, in part because there is no scientific basis for these categories. The large crater caused by an eruption can be millions of years old, so a volcano that has not erupted in tens of thousands of years may be dormant, not extinct. Experts warn that calling a volcano extinct or dormant could lure people living on or near a volcano into thinking that they are forever safe from an eruption.

As an alternative, the USGS has developed a nationwide system for characterizing the level of unrest and eruptive activity at volcanoes. Under this system the term "normal" is used for volcanoes in a non-erupted phase; "advisory," for volcanoes that science shows may erupt at some point in the distant future; "watch," for escalating unrest or a minor eruption that poses few hazards; and "warning," if a highly hazardous eruption is imminent or has begun.

Hurricanes

While disasters like volcanoes and earthquakes are caused by changes going on under the earth's surface, other natural disasters are the result of changes in the earth's atmosphere. Hurricanes, tornadoes, and other storms claim tens of thousands of lives each year.

Few events on Earth rival the power of a hurricane. Called cyclones in the Indian Ocean and typhoons in the Pacific, hurricanes have wreaked havoc for millennia. In fact, some scientists believe that a super-hurricane caused by an asteroid may have wiped out the dinosaurs.

Of the hundreds of storms that brew in the tropical regions surrounding the equator, roughly 40 to 50 intensify to hurricane levels, defined as storms with winds of 74 miles (119 km) per hour or higher. In North America, hurricanes most often form over the Atlantic Ocean in the late summer and early fall, when cold and warm air masses collide. These fierce storms build energy as they move over the water, churning sea water into huge valleys and peaks with 50-foot waves (15 m) at their crest. The warm air moving higher picks up billions of gallons of seawater, which it dumps back to Earth as torrential rainfall. Usually, hurricanes continue to build until something disrupts their flow—most often, land. "Hurricanes are special," concludes meteorologist and writer Jack Williams. "You can make a good argument that they are the Earth's most awesome storms."[7] He cites not only the storms' intensity, but also their immense size: "[a] mile-wide tornado is huge, [but] a 100-mile-wide hurricane is small. Few tornadoes last even an hour; hurricanes easily can last more than a week."[8]

Tornadoes

Compared to hurricanes, tornadoes are small storms, but their winds rotate at a much higher speed—often estimated at 250 miles (400 km) an hour or more. New data from highly sophisticated probes placed in

The Saffir-Simpson Hurricane Scale

A hurricane's intensity is classified according to wind speed using the Saffir-Simpson scale. Developed in the 1970s by Herbert Saffir, a consulting engineer in Florida, and Robert Simpson, director of the National Hurricane Center, the scale classifies hurricanes according to their wind speed and intensity. Storms are given a number between one and five; any storm of category 3 or higher is considered "major"; a category 5 hurricane is considered catastrophic.

Saffir-Simpson Hurricane Scale

Category	Winds	Damage
1	74–95	Minimal
2	96–110	Moderate
3	111–130	Extensive
4	131–155	Extreme
5	155+	Catastrophic

the path of tornadoes reveals that the pressure inside the tornado drops lower than anyone had anticipated, explaining why and how tornadoes maintain their strength even as they run into resistance from touching ground. A single tornado may touch the ground several different times as it continues across the landscape, leaving a scattered path of destruction in its wake. Tornadoes also often occur in clusters. The spring of 2011 was one of the worst tornado years in history. In late April, an estimated 320 tornadoes were spotted in the southeastern and midwestern United States in just four days. According to National Weather Service records, 321 people were killed during the outbreak. Less than a month later—on May 22—a tornado claimed the lives of 157 people in Joplin, Missouri, making it the deadliest single tornado since modern record keeping began in 1950.

Tornadoes are a relatively unique phenomenon. The vast majority of tornadoes occur in a section of the Great Plains that has become known as Tornado Alley. Although much less common, tornadoes occasionally occur in other parts of the world. Outside of the United States, India and Bangladesh are the two countries with the highest number of tornadoes.

Tornadoes vary in size and shape. Several tornadoes are sometimes spawned from the same storm system. Tornadoes often appear quite suddenly. Most large population areas where tornadoes are common have whistles or other warning systems when a tornado is coming, but tornadoes can travel as fast as 100 miles (161 km) per hour, giving people little time to get out of their way.

Floods, Fires, and Other Natural Disasters

Floods may not be as dramatic as earthquakes, hurricanes, or tornadoes, but they kill more people each year than any other type of disaster. In 1931 hundreds of thousands of people lost their lives when China's Huang He (Yellow River) flooded. (Official counts vary widely, from 800,000 to 4 million.) In the United States, floods in the Mississippi River valley destroy crops, homes, and entire towns, costing millions of dollars of property losses each year.

The onset of some floods can last for days, but flash floods move quickly and happen almost in an instant. In 1976, during the celebration of Colorado's centennial, a 19-foot-high wall (6 m) of water surged between the walls of the Bit Thomson Canyon, killing 145 people within a matter of minutes.

The causes of flooding are many—the storm surge from a hurricane or tropical storm, long periods of heavy rain, and melting snowcaps can all contribute to flood conditions. Human activity that changes the natural flow of water, such as redirecting a river or stream, and the conversion of wetlands for development can increase the risk of flood. Environmentalists and land-use planners Mark A. Benedict and Edward T. McMahon write that human changes to the landscape contributed to massive flooding in the Midwest in 1993, which cost 50 lives and more than $20 billion:

> Changes made to the river system to accommodate agriculture
> and urbanization were likely the principle cause of the great

1993 flood along the Mississippi and Missouri rivers. Levees and floodwalls constructed to control the path of the rivers increased the volume of water that could be held in the channel and thus the magnitude of the flooding when the levees broke. Moreover, approximately 80 percent of the wetlands that existed at mid-century had been drained. This not only reduced their ability to act as a natural storage reservoir for floodwaters it also enabled the water to run off more quickly."[9]

Deforestation, intensive agriculture, and development have increased the vulnerability of people and communities to floods. People also have become more vulnerable to forest fires, as population centers have pushed into what land-use planners call the wildland-urban interface. Forest management and fire suppression methods also sometimes disrupt natural processes, increasing the risk of larger and more rapidly moving wildfires when they occur. In 2003 wildfires in California's San Diego and San Bernardino counties destroyed more than 4,800 homes and claimed 22 lives.

⚛ Stormy Weather

While some people do not think of blizzards or thunderstorms when they think of natural disasters, they can be just as deadly as a category 5 hurricane. In March 1962, for instance, a storm raged for several days in the eastern United States. Huge waves wiped out entire beach communities from the Carolinas to New England, killing 40 people and costing an estimated $500 million in losses of homes, businesses, and infrastructure.

Blizzards usually happen when warm, moist winds from the Gulf of Mexico meet cold winds blowing from Canada. They can knock out the electricity and strand people in their homes for days or weeks. Blizzards can be very dangerous. The wind during a blizzard that hit New York City on March 12, 1888, whipped upward of 75 miles (121 km) per hour, blowing off the roofs of houses and uprooting telephone poles. Hundreds of people died in New York during the blizzard; hundreds more were killed as the blizzard raged from Maine to Maryland.

Avoiding Disaster

Whether a natural event is a disaster often depends on how well people are prepared for a disaster and how they react when one occurs. People need to take care to avoid hazards. Sometimes this may mean avoiding building in areas that are susceptible to a wildfire or flood. At other times, it may mean building structures to withstand an earthquake or high winds. It also means taking appropriate steps when the signs show that disaster is imminent. In order to take these steps, people need to understand the hazards and warning signs.

Scientific understanding of the hazards is a critical first step. "The less we know, the more we have to guard against,"[10] says Michael Blanpied, a USGS seismologist. Scientists from many different fields conduct research of many kinds to expand understanding of earthquakes, volcanoes, hurricanes, floods, and more so that these natural hazards do not become natural disasters.

CHAPTER TWO

Reading the Earth and Its Movement

On Sunday, April 4, 2010, an earthquake struck in Mexicali approximately 40 miles (64 km) south of the US-Mexico border. The magnitude 7.2 quake was the largest event to strike the area since 1892 and resulted in two deaths and more than 233 injuries. It also produced thousands of aftershocks and shifted the earth's crust as much as 10 feet (3 m).

Earthquake scientists said they were not surprised that the quake had occurred. "This is an area with a high level of historical seismicity, and also it has recently been seismically active,"[11] explains a writer at the USGS's Earthquake Hazards Program. As elsewhere, however, even the latest tools could not help scientists predict precisely where and when such an earthquake would occur. Even the world's best earthquake scientists admit they still have too much to learn. "This is a very young field, just a few decades old, really," says Greg Lyzenga, a geophysicist with NASA's Jet Propulsion Laboratory (JPL). "We're kind of flying blind a little bit as we try to find out exactly how these things play out."[12]

> **seismicity**
>
> The frequency of earthquakes.

Like any such event, the Mexicali earthquake drew the attention of scientists. The first mystery to solve was which of the many faults in the area the earthquake had occurred on. Scientists also wanted to know whether the Mexicali earthquake had had an impact on other faults in the area. For many years, scientists had believed that earthquakes occur at random intervals along fault lines, but recent research suggests that earthquakes are more predictable than once believed. Drawing on records of past tremors and computer calculations of fault behavior, researchers theorize that the stress relieved during an earthquake moves down the fault and concentrates in sites nearby, increasing the risk of an earthquake at these sites. Lyzenga offers an analogy between faults and a mattress: "If one person rolls over one part of the mattress, it's going to have an effect, subtle or direct, on someone sleeping a few inches away, depending on how stiff or sagging the mattress is. When a quake happens in one location, it moves the material in such a way that it sends stress to the immediate surroundings."[13]

NASA scientists were among those who studied the Mexicali earthquake to test this theory. NASA jets mounted with high-tech cameras and remote sensors have made several flights over the area. The scientists expect to be able to compare images and data collected over time to detect deformations in the crust, or changes in the shape of the landscape, that occur due to the buildup of stress in the fault.

deformations

Changes that occur in the earth's crust due to the build-up of stress in an earthquake fault.

Earthquake Detection

NASA scientists are but the latest to use technology in an attempt to detect earthquakes. Chang Heng, a Chinese astronomer and mathematician, is credited with inventing the first seismoscope in 132 AD. Chang's tool was a sculpture with eight dragons. Each of the dragons had a bronze ball in its mouth; an earthquake caused the ball to drop from the dragon's mouth. People could not tell how far away the earthquake was or how big it was, but they could tell which direction it was by which dragon's mouth was empty.

Today's electronic seismographs are highly sensitive instruments that bear little resemblance to this early predecessor. The seismograph not only detects ground movement, it also records the intensity of this movement. In earthquake-prone areas, seismographs are placed along the ground and in trenches along fault lines, enabling scientists to have precise measurements of a quake's magnitude. Seismographs also record tiny vibrations deep within the earth—data that scientists hope can help them know more about how the earth moves and the interrelationship of various tremors.

Scientists also use data from seismographs to determine how far away an earthquake is. To do so, they compare the recording of the two types of seismic waves caused by an earthquake: primary waves, or P-waves, and secondary waves, or S-waves. Because secondary waves travel at a slower speed, the difference between the time the first P-wave arrives and the first S-wave arrives enables scientists to calculate how far the instrument is from the epicenter. The greater the difference, the farther away the earthquake is. Seismograph data also can be used to determine the exact point where the earthquake occurred. The exact point underground where the rock has moved or broken to release seismic energy is called the earthquake's focus. The point on the earth's surface directly above this focus is the earthquake's epicenter. The epicenter can be found from the distance data from three different seismograph stations. When used to locate earthquakes, this process is called triangulation.

> ### triangulation
>
> A process that uses data from three seismographs to determine an earthquake's epicenter.

Are Earthquakes Predictable?

One of the reasons that scientists want precise information about the location and intensity of an earthquake is to learn whether there are any patterns that might help them predict future events. Scientists hope that mapping the location of earthquakes, aftershocks, and minor trembling might provide clues about how one event can trigger another.

Measurements of the movement of tectonic plates and changes in fault lines are of particular interest to scientists. Geologists today can

A geologist studies seismograph readings that reveal information about a magnitude 7.9 earthquake off the coast of Sumatra in Indonesia in 2009. Scientists look for patterns in earthquake activity using the location and intensity information that seismographs provide.

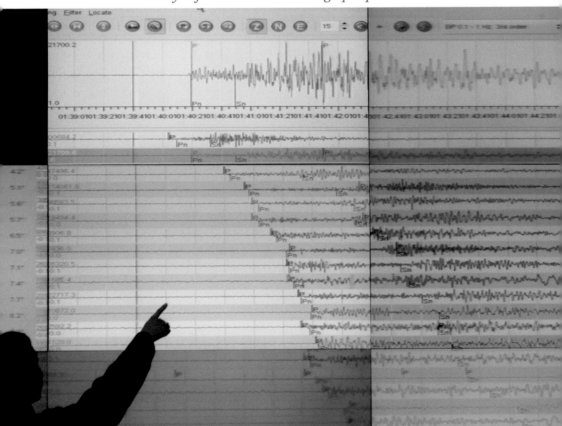

Earthquake Magnitude Scales

Scientists have sought for many years to measure and communicate the power of earthquakes. In 1902 Giuseppe Mercalli, an Italian volcanologist, developed a 12-point scale that quantified the intensity and severity of an earthquake by the observed ground motion and/or the damage it causes. A Level I earthquake causes no damage and little shaking; a Level XII causes catastrophic damage. Later scientists improved on the Mercalli scale, which is now referred to as the modified Mercalli scale.

In the 1930s Charles F. Richter, a scientist at the California Institute of Technology, sought a means of mathematically quantifying earthquakes. The resulting Richter scale records magnitude to the nearest tenth, and each number on the scale represents a tenfold increase in an earthquake's intensity; in other words, an earthquake that measures 6.0 on the scale is ten times greater than one with a magnitude of 5.0. The Richter scale has no maximum limit, but the highest number ever recorded on the scale took place in Chile on May 22, 1960, measuring a magnitude of 9.5.

Researchers have improved on earlier Richter scales to come up with increasingly precise measurements of an earthquake's magnitude. A scale called the "moment magnitude scale" provides an estimate of earthquake size that is valid over the complete range of magnitudes, a characteristic that was lacking in prior magnitude scales. Today, the moment magnitude scale is the most common tool used, but seismographers usually refer simply to an earthquake's magnitude without making reference to the scale that is being used.

measure the earth's movement more precisely than ever before, thanks in large part to the advent of global positioning system (GPS) technologies. A GPS receiver can map its location by receiving signals from navigational satellites that circle the earth far above the atmosphere. Beginning in the early 1990s, geologists began deploying large networks of continuously recording GPS receivers along the edge of fault lines and using the data from the receivers to measure the movement of tectonic plates. Scientists also use creep meters, instruments that measure the space between two points, to measure whether the two sides of a fault are moving away from or closer to one another, and the rate at which the tectonic plates are moving.

Satellites orbiting far above the earth also provide scientists with invaluable information about changes in the earth's surface. Images taken from space sometimes reveal deep trenches in the earth's crust that show the exact location of fault lines. Some satellites are equipped with highly sophisticated radar, called synthetic aperture radar (SAR), that takes precise measurements of the distance between the satellite and the surface. The data are then used to create elevation maps that show the surface of the earth. The technology has enabled researchers to take far more accurate measurements that can be updated daily—or even by the minute. Comparing SAR data at the same point over time enables scientists to detect minor changes in the earth's surface that might suggest the advent of an earthquake or volcano.

Predicting Volcanic Eruption

Satellite imagery and data are also useful in the study of volcanoes, particularly those in remote areas where the expense of keeping and monitoring instruments on the ground is impractical. From the data collected by satellites, volcanologists sometimes can discern changes to the shape of the volcano that suggest a buildup of magma and potential eruption. As magma moves up through the volcanic vent, the volcano bulges at the center. Usually, the changes are not noticeable—they are so minor that they cannot be seen by the human eye, but SAR data capture these changes.

New satellite technology also has improved scientists' ability to scan for gases emitted from a volcano. Among these new technologies is the moderate resolution imaging spectroradiometer (MODIS). A spectroradiometer is similar to other radar, but it detects heat waves rather than light waves. MODIS sensors have been placed on two NASA satellites, the *Aqua* and the *Terra*. Sophisticated computers scan the images collected by the MODIS sensors to see if they contain high-temperature heat sources, or hot spots. "These heat sources may be active lava flows, lava domes, or lava lakes," explains Rob Wright, a research scientist at the Hawaii Institute of Geophysics and Planetology (HIGP). "Since MODIS achieves complete global coverage every 48 hours, this means that our system checks every square kilometer of the globe for volcanic activity once every two days."[14]

The technology enables researchers to detect activity in many volcanoes that previously would have gone undetected. A NASA spokesperson explains the benefit of the new technology:

> This process came in handy in 2002 and then again in 2006 when a volcano in Africa erupted with little warning. Now, at the time, 500,000 people lived in its immediate vicinity, so the potential hazard to human life was extremely high. With the MODIS data in hand, researchers were quickly able to establish the lava vent position, which enabled the modelers to predict which direction the lava was flowing and at what rate.[15]

This information, in turn, enabled officials to evacuate the area vulnerable to lava flow, saving countless lives.

Measuring Volcanic Ash and Dust

Following an eruption, satellite imagery also helps scientists measure the spread of volcanic ash and dust. Most of these images are taken from above the cloud, however, and provide little information about the height of the ash plume. Because volcanic ash can clog jet engines and scour a pilot's windows, it poses a significant hazard to planes flying nearby. In 1982 a British Airways jet flew through an ash cloud during the eruption of Indonesia's Mount Galunggung. The ash sandblasted all the surfaces of the aircraft, making it impossible for the pilot to see. More dangerous still, the melted ash coated the interior of the jet's engines, causing all four engines to shut down. To deal with the hazards, many airports ground all flights when a volcano erupts. For instance, the eruption of Iceland's Eyjafjallajokull volcano in May 2010 forced the largest closure of European air space since World War II, disrupting the travel plans of more than 10 million passengers.

To help avoid the costs of such shutdowns, scientists are seeking ways to improve ash detection and measurement. Rather than relying on images from above, new technologies are designed to detect sulfur dioxide,

The massive ash plume resulting from the 2010 eruption of Iceland's Eyjafjallajokull volcano (pictured) endangered aircraft flying nearby. Satellite imagery and sophisticated lasers are among the tools scientists use for measuring volcanic ash plumes and forecasting their paths.

a reliable indicator of ash clouds. Sulfur dioxide also sometimes indicates the presence of ash when the ash cannot be visually detected from space.

Another technology being used to measure ash plume and forecast its path is a pulsating laser with lidar (light detection and ranging) technology aboard NASA's satellite *CALIPSO* (*Cloud-Aerosol Lidar and Infrared Pathfinder Satellite Observations*). Lidar sends short pulses of light through the atmosphere. Some of the light bounces off clouds and particles in the atmosphere and returns to the satellite. The strength of the returning signal provides information about the characteristics of the clouds or particles. The data from *CALIPSO* can be used to measure the height of a volcanic eruption and forecast the path of volcanic ash. Following the Eyjafjallajokull eruption, for instance, images from the *CALIPSO* satellite revealed that the ash was more than 3 miles (5 km) high. "The . . . observations enable more reliable and accurate detection of volcanic ash clouds," adds John Haynes of NASA's Earth Science Division. "These data provided the European advisory centers with better information to use in volcanic ash forecasting and determining safe fly zones."[16] Rather than shut down all flights, flight controllers can use such information to direct pilots safely around and above volcanic ash.

A Real-Life Lab

Not all volcano research takes place remotely. Unlike other types of natural hazards, active volcanoes provide a real-life laboratory for scientists to collect data and test theories. Many volcanologists spend countless days visiting volcanoes, collecting data about the atmospheric and ground conditions.

On-site instruments also provide clues that a volcano is awakening. Volcanologists place seismographs at or under the surface to measure tremors that would suggest the movement of magma. Volcanologists also use a variety of methods to detect and analyze the gases escaping from the opening in the volcano. Even in their dormant state, volcanoes constantly emit gases from deep within the earth. Scientists monitor these gases and measure the heat of volcanic lakes and vents. Instruments called spectrometers measure wavelengths of ultraviolet light, which help scientists analyze the presence of sulfur dioxide and other gases that may

spectrometers

Instruments that measure wavelengths of ultraviolet light that can be used by scientists to detect gases.

signal an impending eruption. They may also help forecast the nature of an eruption. Volcanologists have learned, for instance, that magma with a higher percentage of silica causes more explosive eruptions.

After an eruption, volcanologists visit the volcano to measure the deposits of lava and ash and collect specimens of tephra for analysis. Their observational data becomes an important part of a record of the volcano's history. Scientists with the European Volcanological Society write, "The careful analysis of the history of a volcano is the most important method in assessing the long-term probability of the occurrence of a specific eruption type and its eruptive energy."[17] Detailed records of a volcano's eruptive history also can help scientists predict the likely flow of lava and volcanic ash.

Ocean Monitoring

Not all hazards are on land. Some of the most dangerous hazards occur on or near water. The expanse of the earth's oceans can make monitoring these hazards particularly challenging for scientists. In many places, coastal tide gauges are the only way to detect a tsunami. Tide gauges are primarily used to monitor sea level and tides for navigation purposes, but scientists at tsunami warning centers also use this data to confirm the generation of a tsunami and predict where the waves might strike. While specially designed tide gauges can be used to spot a tsunami close to shore, they cannot measure the tsunami as it builds energy in the center of the ocean.

Scientists are working to better understand the relationship between earthquakes, volcanoes, landslides, and the tsunamis that sometimes result from them. Huge databases have been established at the National Geophysical Data Center in Boulder, Colorado, the Tsunami Laboratory in Russia, and other smaller research centers to record and analyze tsunamis. Because few sensors are on the ocean floor, underwater earthquakes go largely undetected. Scientists thus have to work backward, looking at the pattern and path of a tsunami's waves to try to detect where and when an earthquake happened. Looking at data from tsunamis that are over 100 years old continues to provide scientists with clues about changes that have taken place under and above the water and how these impact the size and intensity of a tsunami wave.

Scientists have sought to improve tsunami detection. For instance, new undersea seismometers along the Pacific Rim can almost instantly

How a Tsunami Forms

In deep ocean, tsunami waves may appear only a foot or so high. But as they approach the shoreline and enter shallower water they slow down and begin to grow in energy and height. The tops of the waves move faster than their bottoms do, which causes them to rise precipitously.

A tsunami's trough, the low point beneath the wave's crest, often reaches shore first. When it does, it produces a vacuum effect that sucks coastal water seaward and exposes harbor and sea floors. This retreating of sea water is an important warning sign of a tsunami, because the wave's crest and its enormous volume of water typically hit shore five minutes or so later. Recognizing this phenomenon can save lives. In the 2004 Indian Ocean tsunami, an 11-year-old British girl on vacation with her family in Indonesia recognized the ocean's sudden withdrawal as a potential sign of a tsunami, which she had learned about in school. She convinced her family to flee the beach area, saving their lives.

pinpoint an earthquake's location. Complex computer programs then use data about the earthquake's size and location to calculate how long a tsunami triggered by the earthquake would take to reach shore.

These instruments have limitations, however. The seismometers can tell that an earthquake occurs, but they do not provide information about whether a tsunami has resulted or the size or direction of this tsunami. Every tsunami has unique wavelengths, wave heights, and directionality, which hinders accurate forecasting. Warnings may be issued for tsunamis that never materialize. "Partly because of these data limitations, 15 of 20 tsunami warnings issued since 1946 were considered false alarms because the tsunami that arrived was too weak to cause damage,"[18] explain scientists at the National Oceanic and Atmospheric Administration (NOAA).

New Tsunami Detection Technology

Scientists and engineers from around the world hope that new tsunami detection technology will provide advanced notification of tsunamis as they form. New DART (deep-ocean assessment and reporting of tsunamis) systems consist of an anchored recorder on the bottom of the ocean and a companion moored surface buoy. The deep-ocean monitors measure water pressure every 15 seconds; a change in pressure suggests a tsunami wave is passing by. The device converts pressure readings into estimates of sea-surface height, giving researchers an idea of how big the waves will be. Acoustic chirps transmit the measurements to the buoy at the ocean surface, which in turn relays the information via satellite to NOAA's Tsunami Warning Centers, the National Data Buoy Center, and the Pacific Marine Environmental Laboratory. As a tsunami moves across the ocean, comparing the data from different DART buoys gives insight into the speed at which the tsunami is traveling, enabling researchers to predict the time and location of landfall. NOAA explains, "The result is an increasingly accurate forecast of the tsunami that can be used to issue watches, warnings or evacuations."[19]

Although the system works well, it has limitations. There remain some countries that are not part of the warning system. And, even for those that are, the warning system does not always provide enough time

A surface buoy that forms part of the DART tsunami warning system is readied for deployment in the Indian Ocean. The system provides continuous pressure measurements, which help researchers determine the size and speed of waves.

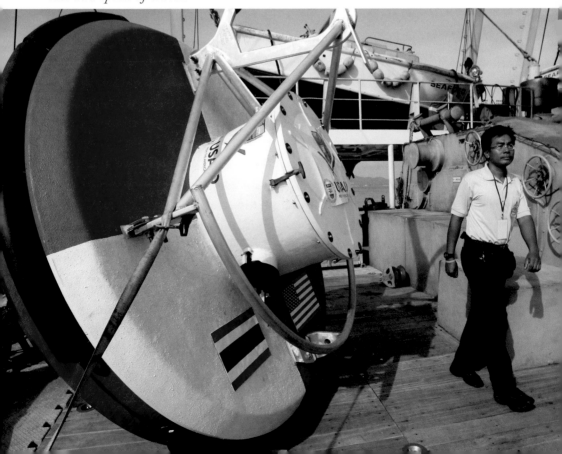

for people on the coast to react. When the 2011 tsunami occurred off the coast of Japan, for instance, local earthquake monitoring systems combined with data from DART buoys to provide immediate notification of the impending disaster. Warnings went out within three minutes of the underwater earthquake, but along parts of the Japanese coast, the waves arrived just 10 minutes later, providing too little time for coastal populations to evacuate.

The Role of Engineering

Because Japan has a long history of tsunamis, it has invested in huge seawalls along parts of the coast. In some areas, enormous floodgates are automatically triggered to close when a seismograph measures significant shaking. Some of these floodgates were too small to stop the 2011 tsunami; others did not close properly. The floodgates at the town of Rikuzentakata failed to shut automatically when the 2011 tsunami threatened. When firefighters tried to close them manually, 45 were swept out to sea. Rikuzentakata was among the many communities that were wiped out from the tsunami that claimed roughly 25,000 lives.

A few villages fared better. In Fudai, a small fishing community on Japan's northeast coast, three of the four enormous floodgates built in the 1980s were closed from a remote site, and workers managed to get the fourth closed just before the first tsunami wave. The gates, which the mayor had insisted be as high as the previously existing seawall, are credited with saving Fudai from devastation. When asked about the floodgate project, a local fisherman said simply, "It cost a lot of money, but without it, Fudai would have disappeared."[20]

Japan's experience shows both the promise and the limitations of engineered solutions. Engineers point out that floodgates like Fudai's work in a narrow valley but are not a good solution for places with a wide expanse of sea. In addition, for floodgates to be feasible, early detection is a necessity. Japan was too close to the earthquake's epicenter for people to be able to respond when the floodgates failed to close.

Engineered solutions also are useless if the earthquake is not detected. If an earthquake in Chile causes a tsunami in Japan, local seismographs will be of little help. To address these risks, scientists are exploring options that could take advantage of the buoys placed in the Pacific Ocean. With proper technology, these buoys could be programmed to set off flares or flashing lights as warning signals. Communications technology may also make a reverse warning system possible, enabling the buoys to send a text message by phone or e-mail to populations that might be at risk.

Regardless of the disaster, increasing the time between when it is detected and when warning can be provided to nearby populations means saving lives. In some cases, particularly with volcanoes, there may be time to evacuate the area before the hazard becomes a disaster; in a tsunami, people may only have a few minutes to seek higher ground. With earthquakes, on the other hand, people typically have no time. Although scientists may be able to say an earthquake will occur along any given fault, they simply do not have any way to predict when the quake will occur. Scientists hope that continuing to study these hazards and expand core knowledge of the factors involved may provide them with the clues they need to accurately predict when the hazard will put people's lives in jeopardy.

Wind and Weather

O n August 20, 2011, the National Hurricane Center issued preliminary public advisories on a tropical storm brewing over the Atlantic Ocean. The winds of tropical storm Irene were not yet strong enough to upgrade it to a hurricane, but satellite images showed that the storm was much larger than average. The clouds around the center, or eye, of the storm were compact and tightly clustered, suggesting that the storm would likely grow in intensity.

Over the next several days, meteorologists at the National Weather Service and local weather stations continued to track Irene. As predicted it grew. Meteorologists at the National Weather Service upgraded it to a category 1 hurricane on August 22, as it moved toward the Caribbean island of Hispaniola; by August 24, it had intensified into a category 3 storm. Day by day, minute by minute, weather forecasters on local and national television displayed models of the storm's likely path and warned residents to get out of the way of what they predicted would be one of the worst storms in history. Using satellite images of the storm, meteorologists measured its diameter at 510 miles (821 km), about one-third the size of the US Atlantic coastline.

Communities from South Carolina to New England prepared for Irene's wrath. Thousands of people were evacuated from the coast and low-lying areas. Forecasters predicted that the hurricane was headed directly for North Carolina and then to New Jersey. New York City mayor Michael R. Bloomberg ordered the evacuation of low-lying areas and shut down the city's subway and bus systems for the first time in history.

On the morning of August 27 the storm made landfall on North Carolina's coast within 10 miles (16 km) of where scientists had forecasted. From there, the storm tracked back over the Atlantic Ocean, picking up water until it slammed into New Jersey, following the path that had been outlined by computer models. Its enormous size also was accurately depicted. It was one of the widest ranging hurricanes in history, impacting 11 different states and causing an estimated $7 billion in damage. New Jersey, upstate New York, and Vermont were hit the hardest. Vermont saw the worst flooding in 75 years; days later residents were still digging themselves out of a thick pile of mud and debris. And all along the East Coast, an estimated 5 million people remained without power for more than 24 hours; some would not see their power restored for over a week.

Intensity Stymies Scientists

Still, the storm told another lesson: For all that scientists know, they still have much work to do. The storm proved to be puzzling in terms of its intensity. Particularly with storms that grow or weaken in strength, forecasts about how powerful they are often prove to be wrong. "What we don't do a good job at is guessing the rapidly changing hurricanes, the ones that rapidly intensify . . . and the ones that rapidly diminish,"[21] says Max Mayfield, the former director of the National Hurricane Center.

A satellite image shows the status of Hurricane Irene the day before it made landfall in North Carolina in August 2011. Meteorologists and other scientists rely on satellite images to assess the size of hurricanes and other storms and to track their paths.

And, when it comes to hurricanes, size matters. "You really do need to know the intensity of the hurricane because the evacuation plan is based on not just where the hurricane is going to hit but on how strong it is," says Mayfield. "There's a big, big difference between a Category 1 hurricane that might have 4 to 5 feet of storm surge versus a Category 5 hurricane that might have above 20 feet of storm surge."[22]

Accurate forecasting of storm surge is important because it is often the resulting flooding that poses the greatest threat to life and property from a hurricane. Severe hurricanes can have a storm surge of 20 feet (6 m) or more. During Hurricane Katrina, which struck the US Gulf Coast in 2005, the majority of the 1,500 lives lost were the result of storm surge.

Data Collection

In the United States, predicting storms falls to the National Weather Service, which is also responsible for generating day-to-day forecasts. Accurate forecasting involves analyzing literally thousands of pieces of data about conditions at the earth's surface and miles into the atmosphere. The National Weather Service has hundreds of reporting stations across the nation, many of which are located at airports. At these stations instruments measure precipitation, air temperature, barometric pressure, wind direction and speed, relative humidity, and other atmospheric conditions.

Precipitation is an important factor in forecasting storms. One of the oldest tools used by meteorologists is the rain gauge, which is used to measure rainfall and other forms of precipitation. A rain gauge has a wide opening at the top to collect rainfall, which is then funneled into a tube that is one-tenth the diameter of the top of the gauge. This seemingly simple tool enables precise measurements to the one-hundredth of an inch. Meteorologists also measure precipitation electronically with a tipping bucket. In the tipping bucket, the funnel leads to two tiny buckets, each of which holds .01 inch (.025 cm) of water. When one bucket fills, it tips and empties. Each tip of the buckets causes the tool to record .01 inch (.025 cm) of rain.

Meteorologists also measure snowfall and other precipitation. The easiest way to measure the amount of snow that has fallen is to place a yardstick vertically into the snow until it hits bottom. In fact, many weather stations have volunteers who use this strategy and/or collect the data from viewers of news weather programs. While this can be a useful tool, it does not provide the precise measurements that professional meteorologists prefer. More precise measurements of snow are generated from allowing snow to melt. Scientists then measure the water and use that measurement to calculate the snowfall; one inch (2.5 cm) of water usually equals ten inches (25 cm) of snow.

Knowledge of the size of raindrops and hail can also be useful in forecasting, particularly when this information is gathered over time. To measure the size of raindrops or hail, meteorologists use an instrument called a disdrometer. Some disdrometers employ laser or microwave technology that also helps scientists know detailed information about the type of precipitation that is falling and compare it over time. Other common meteorological instruments are the thermometer, used to measure air temperature; the barometer, which measures air pressure; the anemometer, which measures wind speed and direction; and the hygrometer, which measures the relative humidity at any given location.

disdrometer

An instrument used to measure the size, distribution, and velocity of raindrops and hailstones.

The Barometer

The first barometer used to measure air pressure was invented in 1643 by Evangelista Torricelli, an assistant of the famous scientist Galileo. Many of the barometers used today are similar to Torricelli's mercury barometer.

A mercury barometer is a simple instrument. A tube closed at one end is filled with mercury and put into a pool of mercury. The greater the air pressure, the higher the mercury will rise in the tube. The air's pressure pushes down harder on the mercury in the dish, pushing more of it up into the tube. A ruler next to the tube records the air pressure. Meteorologists measure air pressure in inches of mercury.

Aneroid barometers have become more common than mercury. An aneroid is a flexible metal bellows that has been sealed after some of its air has been removed.

In addition to these ground instruments, meteorologists use radiosondes to collect data above the ground. First used in the 1930s, radiosondes are weather-instrument equipped balloons that are launched many miles into the sky. As they rise, the instruments collect data about air temperature, humidity, and barometric pressure and transmit the data back to a computer on the ground. In the United States, weather stations launch radiosondes at the same time twice a day, providing a standard way to collect data on weather conditions. The data is sent electronically to the National Center for Environmental Prediction, a supercomputing center that crunches the numbers for National Weather Service forecasts.

radiosondes

Instruments within weather balloons that collect and transmit meteorological data including barometric pressure, wind speed, and air temperature.

To these data collected routinely, meteorologists and hazard researchers add data from tools designed to detect and analyze characteristics of a storm as it forms. Remote sensing instruments are particularly critical for analyzing the movement of weather-related natural disasters because they allow scientists to gain detailed data without getting in the path of the storm.

Radar

One of the most commonly used remote sensing instruments today is radar. The use of radar for forecasting weather came into use almost by accident. During World War II radar operators discovered that rain and other particulates in the air caused echoes on their screen, masking potential enemy targets. The military developed advanced techniques to filter out the data from air particulates, but scientists recognized their value for studying weather patterns. Weather radars send out a beam of energy and measure how much of that beam is reflected back and the time needed for the beam to return. Objects in the air, such as raindrops, snow crystals, hailstones, or even insects and dust, scatter or reflect some of the radio waves back to the antenna. When more of the beam is sent back, the object is said to have a high reflectivity and is indicated by a bright color. Objects that return a small part of the beam have a low reflectivity and are indicated by darker colors. The radar then electronically converts the reflected radio waves into pictures showing the location and intensity of precipitation. Radar can show where the heaviest rain is falling in a hurricane and find storms most likely to produce tornadoes. By the 1950s radar had become a regular and highly useful tool for National Weather Service forecasters.

In the 1980s and 1990s the National Weather Service added a more sophisticated form of radar that measures the Doppler effect, a principle defined by Austrian scientist Christian Doppler in 1842. The Doppler effect can be observed as the change in pitch or tone as sound passes by. In Doppler radar, units beam a signal toward a target and measure how it is altered as it is reflected back. Doppler radar bounced off raindrops or air particles gives meteorologists the information they need to predict the speed and direction of a storm. "Doppler radar allowed scientists to measure motion inside storms for the very first time, providing valuable clues into the development of severe weather," write spokespersons at NOAA. "Using this radar, scientists also discovered that when a tornado begins to form, its winds blow raindrops in a way that appears as a distinguishing pattern or signature on the radar screen."[23]

Doppler effect

A change in the frequency of light or sound waves as a result of movement of the source or the receiver of the waves.

Doppler radar has been particularly useful in helping scientists identify which thunderstorms are most likely to produce tornadoes. "Such thunderstorms often rotate, and being able to measure wind patterns helps us detect this spin,"[24] explains meteorologist Jon Nese.

The National Weather Service operates a network of 158 high-resolution Doppler weather radars called Next Generation Radar (NEXRAD). NEXRAD detects precipitation and wind, processes the data, and displays a map showing patterns of movement that allow weather forecasters to pinpoint storm rotation and better warn citizens of imminent danger from hail, high winds, and tornadoes. Scientists are making enhancements to current technology in an ongoing effort to shorten the time needed between data collection and reporting. Promising advances have been made in this regard, but lengthening the time between when a hazard is detected and when officials and nearby populations are warned of the hazard is an ongoing goal for scientists and others in the field.

Other remote sensing technologies add to a meteorologist's understanding of storm conditions. For instance, meteorologists are making

How Doppler Radar Works

Radar is an essential tool for scientists who forecast and study weather. National Weather Service forecasters were using traditional radar on a regular basis by the 1950s. The more sophisticated Doppler radar was adopted by the National Weather Service beginning in the 1980s.

Both types of radar send out radio waves from an antenna. Objects in the air such as raindrops, snow crystals, and dust reflect some of the radio waves back to the antenna. The reflected radio waves are then converted into pictures that show the location and intensity of a storm.

Doppler radar goes a step further. It helps scientists predict the speed and direction of a storm. It does this by measuring the frequency change in the returning radio waves. The reflected waves of objects that are moving toward the antenna change to higher frequency. The reflected waves of objects that are moving away from the antenna change to a lower frequency. A computer then reads the frequency changes and translates that information into the direction and speed of the storm.

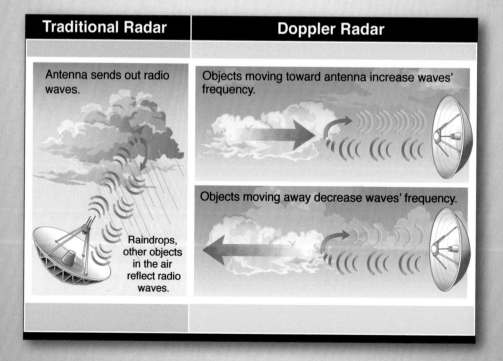

Traditional Radar	Doppler Radar
Antenna sends out radio waves.	Objects moving toward antenna increase waves' frequency.
Raindrops, other objects in the air reflect radio waves.	Objects moving away decrease waves' frequency.

Source: Jack Williams, *The Weather Book: An Easy-to-Understand Guide to the USA's Weather,* 1997.

increasing use of SODAR (sonic detection and ranging), also known as a wind profile. SODAR measures the scattering of sound waves, which can be used to gather precise information about wind speed at various heights. Because data from SODAR is considered unreliable during periods of heavy precipitation, SODAR systems are more useful when studying tornadoes than hurricanes.

Tracking a Storm at Sea

While weather stations provide critical information for detecting severe weather and natural hazards on land, the first indication of a severe weather system at sea often comes from satellites. Satellites provide pictures of Earth from far above, enabling scientists to have a view of an entire storm system. Comparing the satellite images over time enables scientists to track the storm and measure both its path and speed. The size of a hurricane's eye, which is the area of low pressure that fuels the storm, and the formation of clouds around it can provide clues about a storm's intensity. A tightly organized storm is likely to maintain its intensity more than one that appears to be spiraling outward from the eye. Weaker or disorganized storms may also feature an eyewall that does not completely encircle the eye, or an eye that features heavy rain.

The two different types of weather satellites also provide data about conditions that could give rise to a storm. Some satellites, called geostationary satellites, hover over a particular point to collect data on a given area, while other satellites orbit the planet in a north-south orbit.

geostationary satellites

Satellites that remain directly above fixed points on the earth's surface.

The instruments in polar-orbiting satellites gather a wider array of data from a more expansive area. These satellites provide critical data about storms forming over the ocean.

Both geostationary and orbiting weather satellites are equipped with high-tech instruments that collect data about atmospheric temperature, winds, moisture, and cloud cover and beam back measurements in real time. Special kinds of cameras on the satellites also show areas of hot and cold temperatures. The result is a huge database of measurements that meteorologists use to forecast the weather and identify storms as they are forming.

A thermal infrared geostationary satellite image of Hurricane Andrew shows the storm as it approaches landfall south of Miami, Florida, in 1992. Geostationary satellites hover over a specific location to collect data from a given area.

Scientists use data from buoys at sea to provide direct measurements of temperature, air pressure, wind speed, and other conditions. Scientists at NOAA, for instance, monitor a network of 175 continuously operating water level stations along the coast of the United States. These buoys can help predict the storm surge. When a storm threatens, the USGS also deploys water-level and barometric pressure sensors at locations where scientists anticipate a high storm surge.

Hurricane Hunters

Because buoys are stationary, they tend to provide limited information about a storm, so scientists have looked for other ways to get direct measurements. One of the few ways to accomplish this is to fly directly into the path of the storm, a task that falls to teams of pilots and scientists who have come to be known as hurricane hunters.

The first pilot to intentionally fly into a storm was Army Air Force colonel Joseph Duckworth in 1943. Duckworth wrote of the experience:

> As we broke into the "eye" of the storm we . . . could see the sun and the ground. Apparently the "eye" was like a leaning cone as observation of the ground showed a considerable ground wind. . . . On the whole, neither flight through the hurricane was as uncomfortable as a good, rough thunderstorm. Rain had been encountered in thunderstorms which was heavier than the rain in the hurricane, to say nothing of much more severe drafts and choppy and bumpy air.[25]

This first flight became a harbinger of things to come. During World War II, with airplanes that had more horsepower and flew at higher altitudes, regular flights into storms became possible. Today, two organizations have hurricane hunting teams in the United States: the US Air Force Reserve, which uses specially equipped C-130 aircraft, and NOAA, which uses the old navy P-3 planes that have been proven to withstand intense winds. Both fleets of turboprop planes are tough enough to withstand tough winds, but pilots still need special skills to know how to get into and out of a storm safely.

On a typical flight, pilots fly the planes directly into the storm to the eye at its center and out the other side. They do this not just once, but 6 or 7 times. In all, a flight can last 8 to 10 hours. In addition to the pilots and navigators, the flight crew on hurricane missions includes weather specialists who are highly trained to operate in hurricane conditions.

The planes flown into hurricanes are not ordinary turboprops; they are equipped with state-of-the-art technology. A variety of instruments takes measurements of atmospheric conditions and beams the information back to the onboard scientists. NOAA planes, for instance, have radar systems on the nose, belly, and tail of the plane. David Tennesen, who pilots NOAA aircraft, says, "We're actually in a flying weather station. This aircraft has just about every kind of weather instrument you can think of sewn into it and a whole bunch of experimental weather instruments as well."[26]

To complement the data gathered by instrumentation aboard the aircraft itself, the crew drops dropsondes directly into the storm. A variation on a radiosonde, a dropsonde is an instrument package attached to a small parachute. On their way down, dropsondes measure wind speed and direction, temperature, air pressure, and other storm characteristics twice every second, relaying this data back to the crew. The scientists on board the aircraft transmit the data to the National Weather Service and conduct a preliminary analysis that enables the pilot to know where in the storm additional data should be sought.

dropsondes

Instruments that are dropped into a hurricane or other storm to collect and transmit data on the pressure, wind speed, and temperature within the storm.

Storm Chasers

Hurricanes are not the only storms that scientists meet head on; they also seek to learn more about tornadoes by getting an up-close view. In May 2009, for instance, an international team of roughly 100 scientists headed to the Great Plains in hope of catching a tornado in action. They spent the better part of two months traveling hundreds of miles in customized vehicles designed to withstand gale-force winds and torrential rains. The vehicles were equipped with Doppler radar and some of the most advanced scientific technology available. When their instruments detected a storm brewing, the scientists headed toward the storm to surround it with probes and weather balloons. Data from these on-the-ground weather teams was complemented by sophisticated instruments in UAVs, unmanned planes that were tethered to ground vehicles and operated by remote control.

These scientists were part of the largest and most ambitious tornado research project in history, VORTEX2. Spearheaded by the National Science Foundation and NOAA, the $12 million project drew some of the most knowledgeable and experienced scientists in the world. VORTEX2 scientists aimed to view the entire life cycle of a tornado for the first time. Justin Walker, a scientist working on the project, describes how the project differs from other storm chasers: "Normally we all go out on our own, we don't collaborate together on a single storm. [We can] still get good data, but . . . the whole point of Vortex 2 is getting all these vehicles out on one storm so we can have kind of the ultimate data set to really understand tornadoes."[27]

A Hurricane Hunter in Action

Stanley Czyzyk was working as a meteorologist for the National Weather Service in Michigan when he went to an IMAX film called *Storm Chasers* with his family. "I saw the hurricane hunters in the movie and thought that that would be a very interesting job to have," he says. When he saw a job opening at MacDill Air Force Base in Tampa, Florida, for working with the hurricane hunter team, he jumped at the chance to pursue his dream.

Today, Czyzyk is a meteorologist with the NOAA team known as "hurricane hunters." When a hurricane is threatening, Czyzyk boards the NOAA plane that will fly directly into the eye of the storm. As flight director, he is responsible for serving as the liaison between the pilots and the scientists who are collecting data about the storm. This is a job that requires extensive knowledge of hurricane behavior since it is the flight director who balances the need to gather data with the need for keeping everyone safe.

Czyzyk loves his job. "I knew the meteorology of the job would be great," says Czyzyk. "It actually is better than I thought, especially with being able to work with the top scientists in a variety of fields in meteorology, air chemistry, and remote sensing."

Stanley Czyzyk, "Hurricane Hunter," Virtual Career Quest, *USA Today* Education. www.usatoday.com.

Tornado Detection and Warning

Following up on the data collection effort, scientists are proceeding with the analysis, looking for clues about how, when, and why tornadoes form, and why some are more violent and long lasting than others. NEXRAD has helped dramatically improve the accuracy and lead times of tornado warnings, but science still has a long way to go. In some areas, more than three-quarters of the tornado warnings issued by local authorities prove to be unfounded. "One of the things we want to do is lower the false alarm rate," says Walker. "And also increase the warning time."[28] Ultimately, improving the warning system could save countless lives.

Not all tornadoes are detectable or traceable on even the most sophisticated radar technology available. To compensate, many localities in the

Midwest use local storm spotters. Often volunteers, storm spotters are trained to recognize a tornado within a storm system. The storm spotters are linked directly to a local Weather Service office, which can then issue a warning.

Every year, scientists are finding new ways to learn about storms without getting in their paths. As advances in technology continue, the body of knowledge about storms will increase. This body of knowledge is fueled by an immense amount of data, captured at weather centers and in computer databases around the world.

Mapping and Modeling

On January 12, 2010, a 7.0 magnitude earthquake struck 16 miles (26 km) from Haiti's capital city of Port-au-Prince. Intense shaking was felt as far away as Cuba, more than 200 miles (322 km) from the epicenter. The earthquake caused massive devastation. Few of the buildings in Haiti were built to withstand an earthquake, and poorly constructed buildings simply crumbled. According to official estimates of the Haitian government, 316,000 people were killed and 300,000 were injured. More than 1.3 million people were left homeless.

Within a month of the earthquake, teams of scientists from the USGS visited Haiti to study the situation. The first team of seismologists took an initial assessment of the earthquake damage and placed seismographs along the fault where the earthquake had occurred to measure the aftershocks, which proved to be numerous and intense. Scientists used the data from the seismographs to map the aftershocks.

The USGS then sent a team of geologists to map all of the active faults and identify regions at risk of landslides. GPS measurements helped scientists calculate the accumulation of stresses on the geological faults in the area. All of this information was used to create earthquake hazard maps, which use color coding to provide a view of the areas that are more and less vulnerable to ground shaking.

The resulting map is intended to be used as a guide in the rebuilding process. Walter Mooney, a seismologist on the team that visited Haiti, explains:

> The safest places to rebuild are going to be near hard rock sites. Hard rock is stable and has less shaking during an earthquake. While the worst place to build will be those regions with soft sediments and a shallow water table. Both of these we can determine quite easily. Another geological factor is proximity to the fault zone. As you can imagine, the closer you are to an active fault, the stronger will be the ground shaking.[29]

Haiti's capital of Port-au-Prince lies in ruins after a 7.0 magnitude earthquake that struck in January 2010. After the quake, teams of scientists arrived in Haiti to measure aftershocks and map active faults to assist Haitians in the rebuilding process.

The process of mapping the vulnerability to earthquakes and other hazards has evolved over many years. The earliest maps were developed to identify floodplains.

Floodplain Mapping

Essentially, a floodplain is an area of relatively level land that is covered with water from time to time. Experts use years to describe floodplains: A 100-year floodplain is expected to flood once every 100 years; a 10-year floodplain would flood every 10 years. Floods are not this predictable, however; a 100-year floodplain could have two years of flooding in a row. Another way of looking at these numbers is that, in any given year, a 100-year floodplain has a 1 in 100 chance of flooding; a 10-year floodplain would have a 1 in 10 chance of flooding.

Floodplains come in various sizes and shapes. Some are extremely wide and have loosely defined boundaries; others are narrow, linear areas running through a canyon or between two rivers. A floodplain may border a stream, lake, or river, but it also could be a broad, low-lying plain where water runs off from higher elevations.

In the middle of the twentieth century, scientists first began mapping floodplains as part of an ongoing initiative to determine flood insurance rates. Scientists at FEMA, which oversees the Federal Insurance Rate Map (FIRM) program, began with topographical maps that had been developed by the USGS in the 1940s. To create floodplain maps, FEMA researchers added detailed measurements of land and water features and flow, taken by remote sensing and on-the-ground field surveys. The resulting maps were intended to provide consistent data to set rates for flood insurance, but they also provide an invaluable tool for government officials and land-use planners to direct development away from floodplains. "FEMA's Flood Insurance Rate Maps (FIRM) are an excellent example of how we use mapping sciences and hazard models in implementing public policy," writes a course director at FEMA. "The FIRMs are tools that local communities use to guide local land use and other mitigation efforts."[30]

> **floodplain**
>
> An area that is in the path of water as it flows naturally from higher to lower elevations during snowmelt or heavy periods of precipitation.

FEMA's early floodplain maps had a number of limitations, however. Flood estimates were often calculated using just 20 or 30 years of information about peak flow, defined as the maximum height of waterways running their normal course. This provided little information to calculate 50-year or 100-year floodplains. The maps also were expensive and time-consuming to update, so the information quickly became outdated as new structures were built in the areas surrounding the floodplains. Any alteration of the land nearby or upstream, such as a shopping center or parking lot, can potentially affect the ability of the watershed to handle water, thus impacting the levels of the periodic floods. "The height of floods is profoundly increased by building levees, wetland loss, deforestation, stream channelization, and changes in land use," explain experts at the University of Wisconsin's Disaster Management Center.[31]

Floodplain Maps in Action

Historically, many towns have been built near waterways. Floodplains tend to be flat areas with rich, fertile soil, making them highly desirable for agriculture. But building on floodplains has been shown time and again to be a deadly and expensive proposition. Addressing the risk of flooding too often means expensive feats of engineering that redirects the path of water rather than plans that redirect development away from the natural flow of water. Following floods, some entire communities have been relocated to higher ground to avoid a recurrence. Researchers believe that hazard mapping provides a better solution.

For hazard mapping to be useful, however, the resulting maps must be linked to action. Federal legislation on floodplains has helped make this link. In order for flood-prone property to qualify for government-subsidized insurance, a local community must adopt an ordinance that protects the floodway and requires that new residential structures be built in areas at or above the 100-year flood level, as identified by the National Flood Insurance Program. State and local governments are increasingly using the floodplain maps for land use and zoning decisions, natural resource management decisions, transportation planning, and hazard management.

FEMA's flood maps are used an estimated 30 million times annually in the private and public sectors. Community planning officials use them to determine zoning regulations, land developers use them for situating new developments, and engineers use them to develop infrastructure to protect communities from flooding.

Hurricane Floyd, which made landfall in North Carolina in the summer of 1999, was among the natural disasters that made clear the dangers of inadequate mapping. The hurricane was only a category 2 storm, but it caused $5 billion in damage and killed 56 people, largely due to inland freshwater flooding. "At the time, FEMA's flood maps were grossly out of date," writes hazards scholar David Butler. "The explosive development in North Carolina over the two previous decades had made the rivers vulnerable to flash flooding in areas that were perceived to be outside of hazard zones. The rain inundation in the state caused major flooding, enveloping entire towns in some places."[32]

Recognizing the limitations of current mapping strategies, FEMA researchers have created new digital maps. The digital format enables updates to be made regularly, reducing the risk that emergency managers and others will be acting on outdated information. In addition, digital data and maps are more easily used as inputs for computer analysis and modeling.

Geographic Information Systems

In addition to digital data, scientists mapping hazard risks have benefited greatly from geographic information systems (GIS). Put simply, a GIS combines layers of spatial information about a place to enable a better understanding of that place.

Map overlay was one of the first uses of GIS. In this process, researchers select different types of maps showing different aspects of a given place and then put one map on top of another to identify the features of any given site. Which information layers are used depends on the purpose of the mapping process. Hazard mapping usually begins with scientific information about the topography and geology of the land. To help model flooding, for instance, scientists would use data about soil types, drainage basins, water features, and land contours. To see the impact on human communities, researchers would add layers showing utility lines, roads, bridges, and buildings.

> **geographic information system**
>
> A computer system for integrating, storing, and using information describing places and features on the earth's surface.

While the map overlay process can be done by hand, computers have greatly increased the usefulness of the overlay process. In addition to enabling more overlays to be used, scientists can use computer modeling software to simulate complex variations in the earth's topography, precipitation or temperature, and other factors that may influence a natural disaster. Scientists can change the input of one variable to see how that might impact the region being studied. For instance, a researcher can change water level figures that might result from rechanneling a waterway to see the impact on floodplains.

Computer Models Recreate Dangerous Conditions

Scientists at the US Army Corps of Engineers have created software that enables them to recreate the impact of rainfall on a watershed. Scientists input data about the watershed and its features, such as the topography of the land and waterways. Analysts then can input data on precipitation, and the computer will show what would happen—how much of the rainfall could be absorbed into the soil and how much it would contribute to a rise in water levels. Automated calculations also can help researchers to determine the extent and depth of flooding. A similar process is used by scientists at the National Weather Service to model the storm surge from a hurricane. The National Weather Service has created specialized storm surge software called SLOSH (Sea, Lake, and Overland Surges from Hurricanes) that enables them to predict storm surge based on the amount of precipitation, seawater levels, tides, and a host of other factors.

Scientists at the Center for Tsunami Research at NOAA's Pacific Marine Environmental Laboratory also use computer modeling to predict wave heights of a tsunami caused by an earthquake under the Pacific Ocean. Because direct measurements of the ocean's floor are nearly impossible to generate, scientists use computer models to simulate the earthquake and resulting tsunami. Following a real event, scientists work backward, using the path of the tsunami to identify the epicenter of the quake. Each event provides a new set of data to test assumptions in the computer model and tweak the model for increasing accuracy.

In 2003 a magnitude 7.8 earthquake on the ocean shelf near the Alaskan Rat Islands enabled researchers an opportunity to test their modeling methodology. Three tsunameters near the site of the earthquake detected the huge waves that resulted from the earthquake; within 15 minutes of the earthquake, data about the earthquake's magnitude and location were input into the model database to forecast the tsunami's direction, intensity, and point of landfall. The resulting comparison of the forecast from the computer model with that of the real event demonstrated that the amplitude, arrival time, and periods of the tsunami were remarkably accurate.

tsunameters

Instruments placed on the ocean floor that use a sophisticated pressure gauge system to detect tsunamis.

Creating an Earthquake Model

Modeling is not always as simple as taking data and inputting it into a computer software program. Sometimes the difficulty lies in collecting the data. Generating precise data about what is happening under the ocean or land can be difficult.

Scientists have long known that Seattle, Washington, lies directly above a complex series of faults. In fact, several small and moderate quakes have occurred there over the past few decades. In the late 1990s, researchers from the University of Washington decided they wanted a better understanding of how a major quake would impact the city. The first step was to get information about the earth on which Seattle was built.

To get this information the research team used radar-equipped "air guns" to send out a sound source from their research vessel in Puget Sound just off the coast of Seattle. They then used seismometers to gauge the effect of the radar waves. By measuring the waves as they moved through the earth, the team got a picture of what the earth looks like under Seattle. "As the sound waves go down and it hits a different density of rock, we can kind of model what the rocks are like beneath the surface,"[33] says Bill Steele, a researcher at the University of Washington.

The resulting model was perhaps disheartening to Seattle's residents. The city is not built on strong bedrock but instead on loose gravel that would crumble in a quake, increasing the resulting devastation. "The scenario itself is pretty grim," concludes oceanographer Frank Gonzalez. "If you were to have an earthquake on the Seattle fault, the first thing would be widespread destruction just from the earthquake itself."[34] Because the fault line lies under Puget Sound as well, Seattle is also vulnerable to a tsunami. Unfortunately, despite their best efforts, scientists still have no way to predict when the next earthquake will happen. "I know an earthquake is going to happen here in Puget Sound," says Gonzalez. "It could happen tomorrow, it could happen in a thousand years."[35]

Creating Realistic Disaster Scenarios

Since then, a number of other research teams have been building on this model to determine Seattle's risk. The USGS produced a series of earthquake hazard maps that show the relative vulnerability of buildings in various areas. In addition, the Earthquake Engineering Research

Institute, a nonprofit membership and research organization, brought together a multidisciplinary team of scientists, geologists, engineers, emergency response professionals, economists, and social scientists to develop a scenario that models what would happen if a magnitude 6.7 earthquake occurred on the Seattle fault. The team began with existing information, including FEMA's HAZUS (HAZards United States) natural hazards loss estimation software and seismic and geologic maps from the USGS, and then used GIS to relate hazards to Seattle's infrastructure. The study team concluded that an earthquake of this magnitude would cost roughly 1,600 lives and $33 billion in losses.

Building on this process, the Earthquake Engineering Research Institute has developed similar scenarios for the Hayward Fault, which underlies major population areas in Northern California, and the New Madrid seismic zone, which encompasses parts of four states along the Mississippi River.

The New Madrid zone is of particular interest to some researchers because less is known about earthquake risks there. Most earthquakes occur along the edges of continental plates, where plates scrape and collide. In these areas, the faults that result are close to the surface, making them relatively easy to study. But some earthquakes occur in the middle of a tectonic plate, where they are much deeper and more difficult to track. The fault system underlying the New Madrid zone is 4 to 9 miles (6.4 km to 14.5 km) beneath the surface. In 1811 and 1812, this area was the site of three major earthquakes in just three months. Scientists say that if earthquakes of similar magnitude occurred today, they could devastate cities along the Mississippi. Part of the risk is that the seismic waves of earthquakes that occur in the middle of a plate travel farther than those on a fault. In August 2011 a 5.8 earthquake that occurred in central Virginia was felt as far away as Chicago. No deaths and only scattered minor injuries were reported, but the earthquake is a reminder that seismic activity can occur almost anywhere.

Hurricane Models

As with earthquakes, the impact of a hurricane depends largely on its location. For instance, a massive category 5 hurricane that strikes a desolate coastline will do far less damage than a category 1 storm that crashes right into heavily populated New York City. Thus, for scientists to be

El Niño and La Niña

When it comes to storms, no two years are alike. Some years have few natural disasters while others may witness one hurricane after another. Studying the historical record of storm seasons can help scientists understand the conditions that give rise to storms.

One such factor is El Niño. El Niño, which means "little Christ child" in Spanish, was named by South American fishermen who noted unusually warm water around Christmastime. Characterized by unusually warm Pacific Ocean temperatures near the equator, El Niño occurs every three to seven years. When El Niño is present, it affects the position and intensity of jet streams, which can in turn impact the path and intensity of storms. El Niño also typically increases the rainfall occurring near the equator, which contributes to the risk of major flooding.

The complement to El Niño is La Niña, which is a period of relatively cool temperatures. Like El Niño, the presence of La Niña can help meteorologists predict storm conditions. Research has shown that the chances for the southeastern United States and the Caribbean Islands to experience hurricane activity increases substantially during La Niña.

Scientists are incorporating information about these weather systems into computer modeling software. Including such data enables meteorologists to better forecast entire storm seasons and predict the path and intensity of storms as they form.

able to accurately predict the impact of a disaster, they must include information about the population and property in the path of the hazard.

When a hurricane threatens, meteorologists use data collected on the storm to forecast its path. Combining this information with infrastructure and population data of the communities in the path of the hurricane can provide officials, response organizations, and recovery organizations with information about what to expect in terms of damage to key infrastructure such as major roads, bridges, and other transportation networks; phone lines, electricity, and other utilities; and hospitals and other structures. NOAA is among the organizations that lead these efforts. Scientists simply input projections of the specific area where a hurricane will hit, and the computer maps out, within about six hours, what infrastructure is threatened, how much water and temporary housing might be needed, and a host of other factors. The goal is to provide access to this information by government officials to plan and prepare supplies before a disaster strikes. Russell Bent, a computer scientist at Los Alamos National Laboratory, explains, "What we're trying to do is turn those hurricane contours that everybody sees on The Weather Channel into practical predictors for government responders. What we've been moving toward is not only predicting how a hurricane will affect an area but also projecting the best strategies to respond."[36] This research can also help utility companies plan for outages by knowing when and where they are most likely to occur.

Researchers at Purdue University in Indiana have developed a similar system that models a disaster's impact on critical infrastructure, such as roads and bridges, public water and wastewater treatment systems, hospitals, and schools. Makarand Hastak, a professor of civil engineering at Purdue, writes of the model's benefits:

> [It] can be most effectively used as a planning tool before a disaster because it enables you to put preventative measures in place, but it can also be used while the disaster is unfolding to anticipate what will happen next and make decisions about where to evacuate and where to direct disaster relief, as well as after the disaster is over to assess the economic and social impacts.[37]

Using Maps for Disaster Response

In addition to predicting a disaster and its path, researchers also engage in mapping and modeling efforts with response in mind. Satellite imagery from above helps scientists determine the extent of the damage and the areas hardest hit following a disaster. Combined with detailed maps showing hospitals, schools, and other critical infrastructure, this information can be essential to first responders.

When roads are washed away or bridges have collapsed, traditional means of navigation—paper maps or computerized GPS—often prove to be useless. A number of government agencies and private companies have provided software to first responders to use in such situations; advanced technologies are making this information more readily available to a wider variety of people. At GeoCommons.com, for instance, people can access

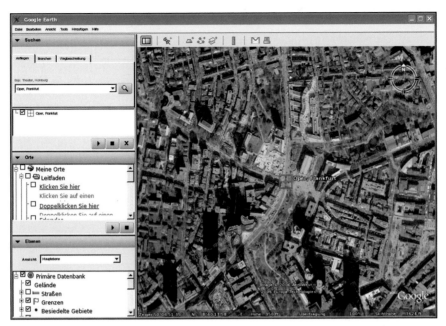

Natural disaster researchers have found uses for Google Earth, the Internet tool that shows satellite views of locations around the globe. Researchers have used this tool to view and assess disaster damage and to help in planning relief efforts. Pictured is a screen shot from Google Earth.

a huge database of maps and add information from their own experiences about road conditions to create their own maps. The maps may outline the extent of flooding, identify roads and bridges that are closed, and provide routes to locations where stores are open. These maps become part of the online repository, available for others in the community to use.

Google Earth also has become a useful tool for disaster researchers, first responders, and victims. Google Earth is a virtual globe, map, and geographical information program that was released to the public in 2005, making satellite views of Earth available to people throughout the world. Researchers have used up-to-date data from the program to view areas subject to widespread disasters. For instance, following the 2010 earthquake in Haiti, Google supplied images that helped disaster researchers assess the magnitude of the damage. Researchers have connected Google Earth with the United Nations to help program analysts see distribution of United Nations–led activities, which in turn can help planners direct disaster relief efforts to where they are needed most.

Today's supercomputers are able to handle an increasing amount of data at ever-faster speeds. Scientists use these tools to develop complex models of how a hazard is likely to impact a community. The results of these complex operations are maps showing the relative risks within a community, models of how people and infrastructure will be impacted, and recommendations for priorities for activities that could minimize a disaster's impact.

New Directions in Natural Disaster Research

For hundreds of years, scientists have been striving to understand, describe, and simulate the many hazards that pose risks to human communities. The process involves constantly fine-tuning the current knowledge of the geology, physics, and chemistry of the earth and its atmosphere. Through research, scientists have been able to improve detection of an impending disaster and provide more people with more timely warnings. But for all that research has uncovered, scientists concede there is still much they do not know.

Hazard research deals with uncertainties. Every hazard—every disaster—is unique. The extent of the disaster depends on conditions beyond people's control but is also influenced by the way people react before, during, and after an event.

Improving Warning Systems

One of the challenges is to improve warning systems for almost all types of hazards. Even with hazards that can be detected well ahead of time, such as hurricanes, preparation is hampered by inaccurate information. Although meteorologists have become increasingly adept at tracking the path of a hurricane, they have not been as successful in gauging the intensity of storms. "To get the intensity right, you have to be able to predict the inner workings of the storm, and that's what we don't do well yet,"[38] says Cliff Mass, an expert on weather modeling at the University of Washington.

In 2010 NOAA and several other organizations embarked on a new research project, the Hurricane Forecast Improvement Program (HFIP). The HFIP website introduces the program:

> The goals of the HFIP are to improve the accuracy and reliability of hurricane forecasts; to extend lead time for hurricane forecasts

with increased certainty; and to increase confidence in hurricane forecasts. . . . The benefits of HFIP will significantly improve NOAA's forecast services through improved hurricane forecast science and technology. Forecasts of higher accuracy and greater reliability (i.e., user confidence) are expected to lead to improved public response, including savings of life and property.[39]

One of the primary tasks of HFIP scientists is to pool knowledge and information currently collected by myriad different organizations worldwide. Scientists can then use this data to create new hurricane models that take advantage of more data. HFIP also hopes to use advanced technology to better track and understand what happens in a storm's inner core.

Unmanned Vehicles

Advanced technology could make it easier for HFIP scientists to achieve their mission. Currently, much of the data collected from within a hurricane is gathered by scientists on specially designed aircraft. Scientists hope one day that the technology will enable unmanned flights as well.

The US military has used unmanned aerial vehicles (UAVs) for reconnaissance missions for many years. Researchers at NOAA and NASA have built upon the military's experience to test the usefulness of UAV technology in civilian areas. NASA has already begun prototype testing of *Global Hawk*, its unmanned probe. In 2010 the VORTEX2 project was among the first to use UAV technology to study tornadoes. The unmanned planes were tethered to a truck equipped with high-tech instruments to collect the data in real time.

UAVs have several advantages over traditional aircraft. Perhaps the most obvious is that they can fly into storms without putting lives at risk. UAVs also are lighter, so they can stay in the air for longer periods of time and fly farther without refueling. This would enable scientists to gather more information about a hurricane's inner workings when it is still far from landfall.

In addition to storms, unmanned aircraft may also be useful for studying other hazards, such as wildfires and volcanoes, where it is neither safe nor practical for piloted aircraft. UAVs also may be useful following a disaster. Following the 2011 earthquake and tsunami disaster in Japan, a team of scientists used a UAV to inspect the nuclear reactors in Fukushima without exposing humans to harmful radiation.

Learning from Animals

In 373 BC ancient Greeks wrote of rats, weasels, snakes, and centipedes leaving their homes in the ground to head for safety several days before a destructive earthquake. Today, eyewitnesses continue to tell of such behavior. In China, for instance, scientists tell of snakes waking from hibernation and slithering out of their dens before an earthquake. Immediately before the tsunami that struck the Indian Ocean in 2004, many zoo animals rushed into their shelters and could not be enticed to come back out, while in the wild, elephants, antelope, and other animals ran to higher ground. In Sri Lanka, where an estimated 25,000 people lost their lives to the tsunami, researchers in the Yala National Park, home to hundreds of elephants, crocodiles, water buffalo, monkeys, and other animals, concluded that not a single animal had died.

While the animals appear to have a sixth sense that a disaster is about to occur, experts say that this is more likely attributable to their keen senses. For years, scientists have been trying to determine whether those sensory abilities can someday be captured and used by humans for detecting natural disasters. Scientists in China have been conducting research on animal behavior in a disaster since the 1950s. In Kenya, Africa, one of the longest-running studies of elephants, the Savanna Elephant Vocalization Project, has been going for 25 years. Scientists hope that these and other studies will uncover how the animals are able to sense a disaster so that they can replicate their sensory ability.

Volcanologist Andrew McGonigle is testing another type of UAV for studying volcanoes. Scientists traditionally use remote sensors to analyze the gases emitted from a volcano. Both sulfur dioxide and carbon dioxide suggest activity within the volcano that may signal an eruption. Scientists usually have to rely on data about sulfur dioxide because carbon dioxide escapes upward quickly, which would require a sensor to be placed directly above the vent. Scientists have looked for a viable way to detect carbon dioxide, however, because it escapes magma earlier than sulfur dioxide. This would enable scientists to predict an eruption earlier than current methods, providing more time for officials to evacuate nearby residents.

To resolve this dilemma, McGonigle has applied UAV technology for use in a remote-controlled helicopter. His *Aerovolc 1* can be flown over the volcano and transmit data to someone operating it from a safe distance. The helicopter is still being tested, but scientists believe it is promising.

Research and Rescue Robots

Not all remote-operated vehicles are in the sky. Scientists have also begun using underwater robots and small remote-controlled research submarines to explore fault lines and volcanoes along the ocean floor. These underwater tools may be equipped with cameras and specialized sonar that let researchers peer into areas that they would not otherwise be able to access. Some underwater robots have collected samples from the sea floor, but one of their principal uses has been to guide response and rescue operations following a disaster. Following the 2010 earthquake in Haiti, for instance, the US Army Corps of Engineers used remote-controlled marine vehicles to help identify damage to and clear debris from Haiti's port. Scientists believe that underwater robots may prove particularly useful in inspecting pipelines, tunnels, and other critical infrastructure following a disaster. Robin R. Murphy, an expert in rescue robots, suggests some of the ways rescue robots could help following the 2011 Japanese tsunami: "Think of all the bridges, ports, pipelines that are underwater! And the missing 10,000 people. Probably underwater. And all in shallow debris filled areas . . . [where] the Japanese Coast Guard can't deploy manual divers. ROV [remotely operated vehicle] and AUVs [autonomous underwater vehicles] are incredible tools."[40]

To the tiny robots available for such operations now, scientists are adding new functionality. For instance, robots that act like snakes could be used to dig through rubble for victims. Daniel Goldman, a biophysicist at Georgia Tech, is working on a sandworm robot that can "swim" through debris to peer into cracks and crevices. To get the correct motion, Goldman used a sophisticated computer model to analyze and recreate

A researcher demonstrates the potential of a snakelike robot that can slither through collapsed buildings in search of victims trapped by natural disasters. Various types of robots are being developed for this purpose.

the movement of a real sandfish lizard. "His latest robot behaves less like an ATV and more like a sandfish lizard, relying on a chain of six motors encased in slick spandex to mimic that animal's undulating motion,"[41] concludes the author of an article on rescue robots in the October 2011 issue of *Discover Magazine*.

Taming Mother Nature

Most of the work of scientists has been to recognize a disaster as a natural part of the world in which we live, but some continue to make efforts to tame nature's fury. For instance, some scientists believe that it may be possible to relieve the stress on a fault with a minor earthquake in order to avoid a larger event closer to a population center. The theory behind stress triggering is that a seismic event, by changing the stresses around it, can make one quake less likely and another more likely, a process that USGS scientists have been studying for years. "My collaborators and I are interested in how one earthquake promotes shocks at some sites and inhibits them in others," explains Ross S. Stein, a geophysicist who has led research on stress triggering. "This work is driven by an attempt to understand the physics of earthquakes, and to develop better ways to make seismic hazard assessments and forecasts."[42]

stress triggering

An unproven process by which scientists might prompt an earthquake in one area to relieve stress along the fault in another.

Some scientists believe that stress triggering could provide a way to control earthquakes or the collapse of a volcano's flank that is caused by such stresses. Scientists know that quakes sometimes result from water pushing apart the two sides of a fault. Some have suggested that injecting water or steam into a fault that appears unstable may offer a way to gradually release the stress and thereby minimize the force of the earthquake.

"This kind of human-induced slip happens at very small scales all the time at geothermal plants and other locations where water is pumped into the earth,"[43] explains Peter Cervelli, who has studied the impact of stress on the Hawaiian volcano Kilauea:

> But when it comes to volcanoes, the extreme difficulty lies in putting the right amount of fluid in the right place so as not to inadvertently generate the very collapse that is meant to be

avoided. Some geophysicists considered this strategy as a way to relieve stress along California's infamous San Andreas Fault, but they ultimately abandoned the idea for fear that it would create more problems than it would solve.[44]

But some scientists continue to explore the notion of stress relief with the hope that they might one day be able to safely mimic nature's process to avoid catastrophe.

To minimize the impact of a volcanic eruption, scientists also are exploring the possibility of using seawater to cool lava as it flows down the slope of the volcano. Engineers also are looking at the possibility of erecting barriers to protect communities near an active volcano from the risk of an eruption. Scientists and engineers are also exploring the feasibility of rechanneling smaller lahars to areas away from people or draining crater lakes to prevent the generation of lahars.

Weather Changes

cloud seeding

The technique of scattering silver iodide, dry ice, or other substances into clouds to induce rainfall.

For decades, scientists around the world have sought to change the weather. In a process called cloud seeding, silver iodide or dry ice is dispersed into a cloud, where its interaction with natural particles stimulates rainfall. Scientists use similar processes at airports to reduce hail and fog.

Making minor modifications to the weather is surprisingly easy. "In weather modification, the uninitiated think you must make huge impacts on the atmosphere to get a desired result," says Don Griffith, who has led a weather modification company since the 1950s. "But it's actually the opposite. If we just make tiny modifications to existing conditions, little touches here and there, the changes then cascade upward using the existing weather's natural actions, and that's what gets the biggest results."[45]

Atmospheric and Environmental Research, a company that offers cutting-edge research on climate and weather-related issues, is among the organizations studying the potential for applying weather modification strategies to hazards such as hurricanes or tornadoes. Ross N. Hoffman, chief scientist at Atmospheric and Environmental Research (AER), has proposed a complex pattern of heating and cooling the atmosphere to weaken a hurricane or shift its path. "Already he has shown, at least on the computer screen, that small changes in wind and air temperature—in fact, no more than 3 to 5 degrees—could have redirected Hurricane Iniki away from landfall in 1992 and reduced the strength of Hurricane Andrew that same year," writes a researcher in *Discover Magazine*. "His colleagues hope to obliterate tornadoes and eliminate the scourge of drought using everything from lasers to tiny, solar-powered satellites orbiting Earth."[46] Hoffman hopes to be able to find a practical way to put his theory to work. "While I can demonstrate that steering a hurricane is possible using computer simulations, we still don't have a practical way to do it,"[47] he laments.

AER is not alone in trying to manipulate weather to reduce a storm's punch. Astronomer Roger Angel has recommended launching trillions of disks of transparent film into orbit around the earth. The ultra-thin disks would provide enough shade to reduce the sunlight by 2 percent, which Angel believes could reduce global warming and moderate extreme weather conditions.

Tying Theory to Practice

Angel's plan, if put into operation today, would take 20 years and an estimated $5 trillion to implement, but some scientists believe more practical solutions can be found. Perhaps the easiest way to protect people from natural disasters, say many, is to communicate scientific knowledge about hazards to the people who make policy. This is not as easy as it appears.

In 2006 FEMA enlisted Amr Elnashai, a structural engineer at the University of Illinois, to conduct research to estimate the cost and casualties if a magnitude 7.7 earthquake were to occur in the New Madrid zone. Elnashai began by creating a detailed database of more than 600,000 hospitals, bridges, schools, and fire stations in the region. He then added information about the type of rock and soil beneath each structure, details of the structure itself, the amount of shaking that an earthquake would cause in that specific location, and the number of people living nearby. Elnashai then plugged all the data into a computer model designed to simulate a 7.7 quake. According to the computer model, a quake of this magnitude would demolish or seriously damage roughly 715,000 buildings and cause death or injury to 86,000 people. The direct economic losses would total nearly $300 billion.

The next step of the program was intended to help government officials and others identify priorities for infrastructure improvements that would save lives in such a disaster, but in 2009 FEMA scrapped the project due to changes in priorities. Elnashai says, "The bottom line is that there is increased awareness, and not much else. Our task was to run the numbers and simulate the effects, and that's what we've been doing. The results are haunting, but they are just pushed aside. An earthquake in New Madrid is a matter of when, not if."[48]

An advisory group of geologists, seismologists, and engineers recently brought together by the USGS concurs with Elnashai's findings. In a 2011 report, the group concluded that the chance of the New Madrid region experiencing an earthquake of magnitude 6.0 or higher sometime in the next 50 years is between 25 and 40 percent. The panel called for the earthquake risk to be "accounted for in urban planning and development,"[49] but few midwestern cities have any earthquake codes or standards in place. Elnashai warns,

> There are no dedicated programs to strengthen facilities or infrastructure in the Midwest in order to resist New Madrid–type earthquakes. Politicians are worried about floods, hurricanes, and tornadoes—things that happen frequently. [Earthquakes] are low probability and high consequence, and politicians only hope they don't happen on their watch.[50]

Disaster-Proof Design and Materials

Research has shown that earthquake-proofing structures can and does save lives. Walter Mooney was on a research team assessing the damage to buildings following the 2010 quake in Haiti. "We . . . found that well-engineered buildings did not suffer much damage. [This is] good news because it means that even though the destruction was very widespread, if the buildings are designed properly, they will survive these kinds of earthquakes."[51]

New disaster labs are springing up that enable researchers to test building design and materials by recreating disaster conditions in a controlled environment. These labs generally document their findings and share them with the hope that they will be used by government agencies and other organizations involved in writing and enforcing building codes and other standards.

Burn chambers—essentially large rooms where fires can be set—are perhaps the oldest type of research lab. In these laboratories, researchers watch fires to better understand how forest fires are powered and to test fire retardant materials. One new material that has come out of this research is a new class of water-based gels that thicken water and help it stick to the roof of a house threatened by an approaching fire.

> ## burn chamber
>
> Within a laboratory environment, a large room where controlled fires can be set to test new building materials or train firefighters.

Simulations and Tests

Several entrepreneurial insurance companies have developed their own laboratories to test building materials. FM Global, a US-based insurance company headquartered in Reston, Virginia, operates a lab in which it can simulate fires, windstorms, earthquakes, and explosions. In 2009 the company spent $40 million to add earthquake simulations to its testing complex. "Today, the new Natural Hazards Laboratory helps researchers further understand what causes building materials to fail and the best ways to design buildings to resist the effects of Mother Nature,"[52] says FM Global's website. The company boasts that, following Hurricane Katrina, the sites that followed its engineering recommendations saw an average of 85 percent less damage than other sites, saving an estimated $1.5 million in losses per property.

The state-of-the-art research center completed in 2008 by the Insurance Institute for Business & Home Safety takes simulations to a new level. In the giant test chamber—which is six stories high and holds up to nine 2,300-square-foot homes (213.7 sq. m)—researchers can simulate hurricanes, hailstorms, tornadoes, wildfires, and other natural disasters. Researchers videotape what happens to different structures during the simulated disasters and then analyze the video to evaluate the quality and strength of building materials and designs. Sometimes, the solutions uncovered in such experiments are surprising. For instance, researchers found that adding a $20 metal strap to fasten floors to walls on a second story can prevent a home from blowing away in high winds.

The center cost $40 million to build, but spokespeople at the Insurance Institute for Business & Home Safety say that it will save the

Lessons from Katrina

Hurricane Katrina, which hit the Gulf Coast in 2005, was the most devastating natural disaster in US history. More than 1,800 people died and more than 1 million lost their homes. The storm is estimated to have caused upward of $80 billion in damage.

Katrina also may be the most widely studied natural disaster in US history. It had an almost immediate impact on the national psyche. People watched in horror as the storm surge broke over the levees and flooded most of New Orleans. Hundreds of people were stranded on the roofs of their homes. Thousands huddled in the Superdome, a makeshift shelter that was not intended to serve this purpose.

Reporter Michael Grunwald echoes the opinions of many when he writes that the disaster could have been avoided:

> The most important thing to remember about the drowning of New Orleans is that it wasn't a natural disaster. It was a man-made disaster, created by lousy engineering, misplaced priorities and pork-barrel politics. Katrina was not the Category 5 killer the Big Easy had always feared; it was a Category 3 storm that missed New Orleans, where it was at worst a weak 2. The city's defenses should have withstood its surges, and if they had we never would have seen the squalor in the Superdome, the desperation on the rooftops, the shocking tableau of the Mardi Gras city underwater for weeks.

Researchers who have studied the New Orleans debacle warn that the very steps that were taken to prevent the city from flooding helped to cause the disaster. Previous researchers had found problems with the levees and predicted that they would fail to hold back rising waters. Ecologists had warned that rechanneling the Mississippi was causing silt to flow into the Gulf of Mexico without being deposited in New Orleans, which was causing the city to sink. Ecologists too lamented the loss of wetlands, which provide an important function of absorbing water. All of these factors may have caused a natural hazard to become a man-made disaster.

Michael Grunwald, "The Threatening Storm," *Time*, August 2, 2007. www.time.com.

insurance industry—and Americans—far more in property damage. Experts estimate that the savings attributable to changes made as a result of this research totaled more than $26 billion in 2009, and they expect this amount to double every decade as the research guides design and construction of residential and commercial structures.

Into the Future

Scientific and technological advances have improved the ability to detect a natural disaster early on, provide warning to affected populations more quickly, and improve the accuracy of forecasts and models showing the potential impact. Improvements in building materials and engineered solutions provide additional protection to people and property. These advances have assuredly saved countless lives. And tomorrow's advances will likely save countless more.

Construction workers rebuild a Southern California hospital damaged by an earthquake. Studies have shown that building design can save lives during an earthquake and disaster labs are helping researchers test building design and materials for real-world use.

But the earth is ever changing. Scientists warn that global warming may create new hazards and new disasters. Experts predict that the gradual warming of the earth will increase the amount of precipitation in some areas. Sea levels will continue to rise with the melting of the ice caps. Hazards experts predict increased flooding both in coastal communities and in low-lying inland areas. Scientists warn also that global warming will increase the number and intensity of hurricanes and other storms.

NOAA is among the organizations with a mission that addresses both climate change and natural disaster research. Its website envisions a future in which the understanding of the natural and man-made forces involved in these two areas coincide:

> Imagine a future where we understand and predict climate trends and variability with a reasonable amount of certainty. Armed with this knowledge, we can make informed decisions that reduce the socioeconomic impact of weather events on the ever-increasing global population and help us live in harmony with the delicate checks and balances of nature.[53]

Disaster research has shown time and time again that natural disasters are a fact of life. They are a natural part of the world in which we live. Whether we are prepared or not, natural events will occur. When they do, scientists will be on hand to study them in the hopes of learning a little bit more. And where these scientists leave off, others will pick up to translate new findings, new lessons, and new approaches into actionable plans to save lives and property.

Source Notes

Introduction: Why Study Disasters?

1. Jose Borrero, "Day 2: January 4, 2005," notes, University of Southern California Tsunami Research Center. www.usc.edu.

2. Claire B. Rubin, ed., *Emergency Management: The American Experience, 1900–2005*. Fairfax, VA: Public Entity Risk Institute, 2007, p. 3.

3. Jose Borrero, "Day 7, 8: January 9–10, 2005," notes, University of Southern California Tsunami Research Center. www.usc.edu.

4. George Pararas-Carayannis, "The Great Earthquake and Tsunami of 26 December 2004 in Southeast Asia and the Indian Ocean," 2005. www.drgeorgepc.com.

5. Quoted in Mark Cantrell, "Into the Eye of the Storm," *Military Officer*, July 2003. www.moaa.org.

Chapter One: What Are Natural Disasters?

6. Quoted in *Inside Earthquakes*, National Geographic video. http://video.nationalgeographic.com.

7. Jack Williams, *The Weather Book: An Easy-to-Understand Guide to the USA's Weather*. New York: New Gannett Media, 1997, p. 131.

8. Williams, *The Weather Book*, p. 131.

9. Mark A. Benedict and Edward T. McMahon, *Green Infrastructure: Linking Landscapes and Communities*. Washington, DC: Island Press, 2006.

10. Quoted in Amy Barth, "Big Idea: A Shock to the Heartland," *Discover Magazine*, October 2011. http://discovermagazine.com.

Chapter Two: Reading the Earth and Its Movement

11. USGS, "Magnitude 7.2—Baja California, Mexico," Earthquake Hazards Program. http://earthquake.usgs.gov.

12. Quoted in Hector Becerra, "Scientists Seek Clues in Mexicali Earthquake," *Los Angeles Times*, July 2, 2010. http://articles.latimes.com.

13. Quoted in Becerra, "Scientists Seek Clues in Mexicali Earthquake."

14. Quoted in Laurie J. Schmidt, "Sensing Remote Volcanoes," NASA Earth Observatory, July 13, 2009. http://earthobservatory.nasa.gov.

15. Jennifer Pulley, "NASA 360: Season 1, Show 8," NASA podcast, March 20, 2009. www.nasa.gov.

16. Quoted in Steve Cole, "NASA Aids Forecasters Tracking Iceland Volcano Ash Plume," NASA News. www.nasa.gov.

17. European Volcanological Society, "Prediction of Volcanic Eruptions," April 28, 2011. www.sveurop.org.

18. Eddie N. Bernard, "The Tsunami Story," National Oceanic and Atmospheric Administration. www.tsunami.noaa.gov.

19. NOAA Center for Tsunami Research, "Deep-Ocean Assessment and Reporting of Tsunamis (DART)." http://nctr.pmel.noaa.gov.

20. Quoted in *Daily Mail* (London), "The Japanese Mayor Who Was Laughed at for Building a Huge Sea Wall—Until His Village Was Left Almost Untouched by Tsunami," May 14, 2011. www.dailymail.co.uk.

Chapter Three: Wind and Weather

21. Quoted in "Hurricane Dust," National Geographic video. http://video.nationalgeographic.com.

22. Quoted in "Hurricane Dust."

23. NOAA, "Tornado Detection and Warnings; Doppler Radar," *NOAA Celebrates 200 Years of Science, Service, and Stewardship*, 2007. http://celebrating200years.noaa.gov.

24. WHYY TV12, "Advantages of Doppler Radar," Franklin Fact Archive, April 12, 2000. www.whyy.org.

25. Quoted in Howard C. Sumner, "North Atlantic Hurricanes and Tropical Disturbances of 1943," *Monthly Weather Review*, November 1943, p. 1.

26. Quoted in Cantrell, "Into the Eye of the Storm."

27. Quoted in MSNBC, "Tracking Twisters: Vortex 2 Heads Back to KS," May 5, 2010. www.vortex2.org.

28. Quoted in MSNBC, "Tracking Twisters."

Chapter Four: Mapping and Modeling

29. Quoted in USGS, "Help in Haiti—The Role of Science," podcast, March 3, 2010. http://gallery.usgs.gov.

30. FEMA Training, "Session 14: Utilizing Mapping and Modeling in Hazard Mitigation Planning and Land Use," p. 14-4. http://training.fema.gov.

31. University of Wisconsin Disaster Management Center, "Flood of Evidence," November 23, 2004. http://whyfiles.org.

32. Quoted in Rubin, *Emergency Management*, p. 50.

33. Quoted in "Seattle Quake," National Geographic video. http://video.nationalgeographic.com.

34. Quoted in "Seattle Quake," National Geographic video.

35. Quoted in "Seattle Quake," National Geographic video.

36. Quoted in Sue Vorenberg, "Staying a Step Ahead of Natural Disasters," *New Mexican* (Santa Fe), July 16, 2009. www.santafenewmexican.com.

37. Quoted in Purdue University News Room, "Model Aims to Reduce Disaster Toll on City's Social, Economic Fabric," September 28, 2010. www.purdue.edu.

Chapter Five: New Directions in Natural Disaster Research

38. Quoted in Alan Boyle, "Experts Review the Lessons Learned from Hurricane Irene," *Cosmic Log*, msnbc.com, August 29, 2011. http://cosmiclog.msnbc.msn.com.

39. Hurricane Forecast Improvement Program, "Improving the Accuracy and Reliability of Hurricane Forecasts," NOAA, 2011. www.hfip.org.

40. Quoted in *Washington Post* Conversations, "Tornadoes, Natural Disasters: How High-Tech Robots Help in Search and Rescue," May 25, 2011. http://live.washingtonpost.com.

41. Adam Piore, "Lesson Learned from 9-11: We Need Better Rescue Bots," *Discover Magazine*, October 2011. http://discovermagazine.com.

42. Ross S. Stein, "Short Biography: Earthquake Deformation, Interaction, and Stress Triggering," USGS Professional Pages, December 2, 2009. http://profile.usgs.gov.

43. Peter Cervelli, "The Threat of Silent Earthquakes," *Scientific American*, September 15, 2008. www.scientificamerican.com.

44. Cervelli, "The Threat of Silent Earthquakes."

45. Quoted in Donovan Webster, "Harnessing the Weather," *Discover Magazine*, June 6, 2008. http://discovermagazine.com.

46. Webster, "Harnessing the Weather."

47. Quoted in Webster, "Harnessing the Weather."

48. Quoted in Barth, "Big Idea."

49. USGS, *Report of the Independent Expert Panel on New Madrid Seismic Zone Earthquake Hazards*, April 16, 2011, p. 1. http://earthquake.usgs.gov.

50. Quoted in Barth, "Big Idea."

51. Quoted in USGS, "Help in Haiti—The Role of Science," podcast, March 3, 2010. http://gallery.usgs.gov.

52. FM Global, "Research: The Natural Hazards Laboratory," http://www.fmglobal.com.

53. NOAA, "The Future of Climate Research," *NOAA Celebrates 200 Years of Science, Service, and Stewardship*, April 25, 2007. http://celebrating200years.noaa.gov.

Facts About Natural Disasters

Earthquakes

- Several million earthquakes occur in the world each year. Many are un-detected because they occur in remote areas or are very weak.
- Roughly 75–80 percent of all the earth's quakes occur along the rim of the Pacific Ocean.
- The magnitude 9.0 earthquake that struck Japan in 2011 was powerful enough to shorten Earth's day by 1.8 microseconds.
- As of 2011, five earthquakes of magnitude 9.0 or higher have been recorded since 1900, when instruments began keeping track.
- The USGS warns that earthquakes pose a significant risk to more than 75 million Americans in 39 states.
- The USGS reports that Alaska is the most earthquake-prone state and one of the most seismically active regions in the world. It experiences a magnitude 7.0 earthquake almost every year, and a magnitude 8.0 or higher roughly every 14 years.

Tsunamis

- A tsunami can be triggered by an earthquake, volcanic eruption, or landslide.
- Most tsunamis consist of multiple waves with powerful currents, in some instances, hitting shore more than an hour apart from one an-other.
- Tsunamis can travel across the ocean at a rate of 500 miles (800 km) an hour.
- Some of the most destructive tsunamis have been the result of earthquakes occurring thousands of miles away. On May 22, 1960, a magnitude 9.5 earthquake off the coast of Chile triggered a tsu-nami that spread throughout the Pacific Ocean and caused about 2,300 deaths.

FACTS ABOUT

- The 2004 Indian Ocean tsunami, considered the deadliest tsunami in history, reached heights of 65 to 100 feet (20 m to 30.5 m) in Sumatra, Indonesia.

Volcanoes
- According to the USGS and the European Space Agency, there are currently about 500 active volcanoes in the world.
- Roughly 75 to 80 percent of active volcanoes are along the Pacific Ring of Fire.
- Worldwide, at least 500 million people live close to an active volcano.
- About 100 aircraft encounters with volcanic ash have been documented between 1973 and 2003. About 20 percent of these resulted in significant damage; in eight of these the damage was so severe that in-flight engine failures occurred.
- Mauna Loa, in Hawaii, is the world's largest active volcano.

Hurricanes
- Hurricanes can travel thousands of miles. Although the intensity may change, hurricanes typically do not die out until they run into land.
- Hurricanes can pick up 2 billion tons of water vapor, which is then dumped on land as torrential rain.
- The most dangerous aspect of a hurricane is often the storm surge, the height of the water above what would be normal for that time. The storm surge can exceed 20 feet (6 m) and extend 100 miles (161 km) along the shore.
- The deadliest natural disaster in US history was a hurricane that hit Galveston, Texas, in 1900. Roughly 8,000 people lost their lives.

Tornadoes
- On average, more than 800 twisters whip through the area known as Tornado Alley each year.
- Tornadoes generate the fastest winds on Earth; they can whip as high as 300 miles (500 km) per hour, but only 2 percent of tornadoes have winds higher than 200 miles (320 km) per hour.
- Tornadoes last anywhere from 20 seconds to an hour.
- According to NOAA, 753 tornadoes occurred in the United States in April 2011, making it the most active tornado month on record.

- According to VORTEX2 scientists, current tornado warnings have only a 13-minute average lead time.
- According to research cited by disaster expert Richard Sylves, roughly 77 percent of fatalities from tornadoes are people in mobile homes.

Floods

- Over 75 percent of declared federal disasters are related to floods.
- According to USGS statistics, floods kill about 140 people each year and cause $5 billion in property damage.
- Loss of life to floods has declined over the past 50 years, but economic losses have continued to rise due in part to increasing coastal populations.

Related Organizations

European Volcanological Society (SVE)

Société Volcanologique Européenne
C.P. 1, 1211
Geneva 17 Switzerland
fax: +41 22 759 2105
e-mail: info@sveurop.org
website: www.sveurop.org

Based in Geneva, Switzerland, the SVE is an independent scientific organization established in 1991 to develop international cooperation researching and forecasting volcanic eruptions.

Federal Emergency Management Agency (FEMA)

500 C St. SW
Washington, DC 20472
phone: (202) 646-2500
website: www.fema.gov

Currently under the Department of Homeland Security, FEMA's mission is to reduce the loss of life and property and protect communities nationwide from all hazards, including natural disasters, acts of terrorism, and other man-made disasters.

National Oceanic and Atmospheric Administration (NOAA)

1401 Constitution Ave. NW, Room 5128
Washington, DC 20230
phone: (301) 713-1208
website: www.noaa.gov

NOAA is a scientific agency within the U.S. Department of Commerce that focuses on conditions of the earth's oceans and the atmosphere.

National Weather Service

1325 E. West Hwy.
Silver Spring, MD 20910
website: www.weather.gov

Housed within the National Oceanic and Atmospheric Administration, the National Weather Service is responsible for collecting data and issuing weather, hydraulic, and climate forecasts and warnings for the United States.

Natural Hazards Center

University of Colorado at Boulder
483 UCB
Boulder, CO 80309
phone: (303) 492-6818
e-mail: hazctr@colorado.edu

The Natural Hazards Center serves as a national and international clearinghouse of knowledge concerning the social science and policy aspects of disasters. The center collects and shares research and experience related to preparedness for, response to, recovery from, and mitigation of disasters.

U.S. Geological Survey (USGS)

12201 Sunrise Valley Dr.
Reston, VA 20192
phone: (888) 275-8747 or (703) 648-5953
website: www.usgs.gov

The USGS is a science organization that collects, monitors, analyzes, and provides scientific understanding about natural resource conditions, issues, and problems. Natural hazards is one of its core research areas.

For Further Research

Books

Patrick L. Abbott, *Natural Disasters.* New York: McGraw-Hill, 2011.

Melanie A. Carmichael, *Earthquake Research: Background and Select Reports.* Hauppauge, NY: Nova Science, 2010.

Damon P. Coppola, *Introduction to International Disaster Management.* Burlington, MA: Butterworth-Heinemann, 2011.

Sarah L. Gilbert, ed., *Tornadoes and Windstorms: Background, Research, and Hazard Mitigation.* Hauppauge, NY: Nova Science, 2010.

Donald Hyndman and David Hyndman, *Natural Hazards and Disasters.* Pacific Grove, CA: Brooks Cole, 2010.

Edward A. Keller and Duane E. DeVecchio, *Natural Hazards: Earth's Processes as Hazards, Disasters, and Catastrophes.* New York: Prentice-Hall, 2011.

Seth Stein, *Disaster Deferred: How New Science Is Changing Our View of Earthquake Hazards in the Midwest.* New York: Columbia University, 2009.

Jennifer L. Viegas, ed., *Scientific American Critical Anthologies on Environment and Climate: Critical Perspectives on Natural Disasters.* New York: Rosen, 2007.

John Withington, *Disaster! A History of Earthquakes, Floods, Plagues, and Other Catastrophes.* New York: Skyhorse, 2010.

Websites

BrainPOP: Natural Disasters (www.brainpop.com/science/earthsystem/naturaldisasters). The BrainPOP website provides free information on tsunamis, hurricanes, floods, and earthquakes. Features include video, activities, Q&A, and quizzes.

Global Volcanism Program (www.volcano.si.edu/index.cfm). This educational website provides a wealth of information about volcanoes and volcanic activity worldwide. The site is searchable by the volcano's

FOR FURTHER RESEARCH

name, region, or eruption date, and provides photos and videos, as well as written information and links to other sites.

NASA Earth Observatory: Natural Hazards (http://earthobservatory .nasa.gov/NaturalHazards). This website provides an interactive world map marking current and recent natural disasters. Click on a hazard to see photos taken by NASA satellites and read a brief description.

National Geographic: Natural Disasters (http://environment.national geographic.com/environment/natural-disasters). This website includes comprehensive information about why, how, and when disasters occur. The site includes articles, videos, and photos.

National Geophysical Data Center (www.ngdc.noaa.gov/hazard). Provides data, information, images, and educational materials on tsunamis, earthquakes, volcanoes, and other natural disasters.

National Hurricane Center (www.nhc.noaa.gov). This arm of the National Weather Service provides a wealth of information about hurricanes, hurricane research and researchers, and forecast models. It also includes a real-time look at hurricanes and tropical storms that may be threatening the US coast.

National Hurricane Center/Tropical Prediction Center: Hurricane and Natural Disaster Brochures (www.aoml.noaa.gov/general/lib/ hurricbro.html). This portal provides access to NOAA brochures covering the science of hurricanes, tornadoes, floods, and other natural disasters.

Natural Disasters: Destructive Forces of Nature (http://library.think quest.org/16132/frames.html). Developed by students for students, this interactive site focuses on tornadoes, volcanoes, tsunamis, lightning, earthquakes, hurricanes, and drought. Features include a chat room, forum, search feature, and quiz game.

NeoK12: Natural Disasters (www.neok12.com/Natural-Disasters.htm). This website provides educational videos, lessons, and games about volcanoes, tsunamis, earthquakes, hurricanes, tornadoes, and other natural disasters.

NOAA Center for Tsunami Research (http://nctr.pmel.noaa.gov/ index.html). This website provides information about tsunami forecasting, hazard assessment, and research, including the innovative DART system.

On Being a Scientist: A Guide to Responsible Conduct in Research (www.nap.edu/openbook.php?record_id=12192&page=R1). This is a free, downloadable book from the National Academy of Sciences Committee on Science, Engineering, and Public Policy. The 2009 edition provides a clear explanation of the responsible conduct of scientific research. Chapters on treatment of data, mistakes and negligence, the scientist's role in society, and other topics offer invaluable insight for student researchers.

Pacific Tsunami Museum (www.tsunami.org). This website includes a wealth of information about tsunamis, including survivor stories and a guide intended for students.

Scholastic: Severe Weather and Natural Disasters (http://teacher.scholastic.com/activities/wwatch/severe.htm). This educational website provides in-depth information about volcanoes, earthquakes, hurricanes, winter storms, and tornadoes. The features include eyewitness accounts, conversations with experts, and suggestions for science experiments.

Index

Note: Boldface page numbers indicate illustrations.

Picture Credits

Cover: iStockphoto.com

Maury Aaseng: 18, 46

AP Images: 11, 21, 29, 33, 37, 41, 48, 54, 63, 69, 76

iStockphoto.com: 8 (bottom), 9 (top)

Photos.com: 8 (top)

Thinkstock: 9 (bottom)

PICTURE CREDITS

About the Author

Lydia Bjornlund is a freelance writer and editor living in Northern Virginia. She has written more than two dozen nonfiction books for children and teens, mostly on American history and health-related topics. She also writes books and training materials for adults on issues related to land conservation, emergency management, and public policy. Bjornlund holds a master's degree in education from Harvard University and a BA in American Studies from Williams College. She lives with her husband, Gerry Hoetmer, and their children, Jake and Sophia.

ABOUT THE AUTHOR